MONOGAMY? IN THIS ECONOMY?

of related interest

The Anxious Person's Guide to Non-Monogamy
Your Guide to Open Relationships, Polyamory and Letting Go
Lola Phoenix
Foreword by Kathy G. Slaughter
ISBN 978 1 83997 213 3
eISBN 978 1 83997 214 0

The Queer Mental Health Workbook
A Creative Self-Help Guide Using CBT, CFT and DBT
Dr Brendan J Dunlop
ISBN 978 1 83997 107 5
eISBN 978 1 83997 108 2

Queer Body Power
Finding Your Body Positivity
Essie Dennis
ISBN 978 1 78775 904 6
eISBN 978 1 78775 905 3

Monogamy? In *this* Economy?

Finances, Childrearing, and Other Practical Concerns of Polyamory

Laura Boyle

Foreword by Libby Sinback

Jessica Kingsley Publishers
London and Philadelphia

First published in Great Britain in 2024 by Jessica Kingsley Publishers
An imprint of John Murray Press

1

A CIP catalogue record for this title is available from the British Library and the Library of Congress

ISBN 978 1 80501 118 7
eISBN 978 1 80501 119 4

Printed and bound in the United States by Integrated Books International

Jessica Kingsley Publishers' policy is to use papers that are natural, renewable and recyclable products and made from wood grown in sustainable forests. The logging and manufacturing processes are expected to conform to the environmental regulations of the country of origin.

Jessica Kingsley Publishers
Carmelite House
50 Victoria Embankment
London EC4Y 0DZ

www.jkp.com

John Murray Press
Part of Hodder & Stoughton Ltd
An Hachette Company

This book is dedicated to Edward and Harper, for listening to me when I told them to get off their screens and went right back to mine to work on it; and to Ken and Emma for their patience in listening to me talk through every block I stumbled on in putting it together.

Contents

Foreword

In 2020, Kyrr (they/them), my partner of five years moved in with me. If I ended that story there, it might sound unremarkable. You might see it as a natural progression of a long-term relationship. But this story has a twist: at the time, I was already living with my spouse of eight years, my two young kids, and my mom.

See, I'm polyamorous. I have multiple romantic partners.

Kyrr (who is also my husband's partner) moved in right after the pandemic lockdown had begun. We'd all been talking about the possibility for a few years, but the pandemic pushed things a bit. They needed to move out of their current place, and it was either in with us or down to Florida to live with their parents. Neither I nor my husband wanted to have a long separation, so cohabiting it was. It was a big step, but given how involved we all were in each other's lives, it just made sense.

My story may sound unusual, but according to research, it's increasingly common. One in nine people have been in a polyamorous relationship at some point in their life, and one in six are interested in the possibility (Moors, Gesselman, and Garcia 2021). Still, since most people who are polyamorous don't talk about their lives or relationships due to fears of stigma or judgment, a lot of people still don't know much about this relationship practice and how it actually plays out day-to-day.

My mom, who also lived with us, has always been chill about polyamory. My spouse's parents however, were a little less comfortable. As with many people, polyamory was just so unfamiliar to them. To them it broke a lot of rules that felt unbreakable. They couldn't wrap their heads around it. They were uncomfortable, concerned, confused, and curious. What we were doing seemed so foreign to them. They worried about the health of our marriage and the wellbeing of our kids.

A few months after Kyrr moved in, my mom told me that my in-laws called her up and asked her "Who sleeps where?"

The "Who sleeps where?" question is a common one. And I get it. If you're a monogamous couple, the presumption is that you are sleeping in the same bed every night. Add in additional people, and it's confusing. That question is probably also a proxy for a whole lot of other questions, like "Who's the most important?" "Do y'all all have sex together?" "How do you handle it if two people are together and one person isn't?"

Another question I get a lot is, "How does this work with kids?" Or some variation thereof. As a parent of two elementary school-aged children, I get people wondering if it is confusing for them: "Are they okay?" "How do they relate to your other partner?" "What do your kids call them?"

These questions are really common ones for polyamorous people to get. When something is unfamiliar and doesn't fit into your worldview, it's hard to understand how it can work. People's imaginations run wild.

The reality is far more boring. My family was lucky enough to procure a five-bedroom house, so everyone has their own room, and we sleep where we feel like sleeping. Our sex lives are private, just like any other family with adults in it. My kids have never known a time when their parents weren't polyamorous, and their parents are open that we love each other, and we also love other people, and none of that is a threat. They don't know anything is strange or unusual—this is their normal.

My non-coparent partner has pretty clear boundaries around childcare and parenting decisions, but it's an ongoing conversation that's not all that different from a step-parent or other family member that might be living with us. It's worth stating that outside of white, Western cultures, there are a lot of cultures in which it is common to live in multigenerational households, with adult siblings, cousins, all sharing household and childcare duties. So if you're having a hard time wrapping your mind around how multiple partners could live together, just think of those partners as extra family members.

I never mind telling clients and friends how my partners and I live. I enjoy their surprise when they realize that the actual challenges we have end up looking more similar to than different from the challenges that any family faces in raising two neurodivergent children in a country that alienates parents, is experiencing unprecedented inflation in the cost of living, and is facing a crisis in both healthcare and public education. We have differences to work out of course. We also have more people willing to do the dishes. What is for certain is that all of us are able to live better together than we would be able to apart.

Of course, though, I worry about the stigma from living and loving differently. I worry about it most when it comes to my kids—what will their friends and the parents of their friends think? Since so little is known about how polyamorous households and families work and what it's really like, it makes sense that people would judge. People judge and fear what they don't understand.

That judgment and fear doesn't just potentially harm me and my family, but as I said, that fear can keep families like mine quiet about what they're doing, which can then prevent people who are interested in creating a polyamorous family or living with their polyamorous partners from having any model of how that can look. Lots of people will tell you polyamory doesn't work, and that it's unnatural or wrong to cohabit with more than one partner. If you don't see any examples of how it can work, you might believe that those folks are right.

There are, though, lots of polyamorous families that are living together and thriving. As a polyamorous educator, podcaster, and coach, I put my life out there in part so that I can offer one model of how this can look. But I'm only one person, and my family only one family.

For this reason and many others, I'm glad Laura Boyle has written this book. Through questionnaires and interviews, she has gathered a wealth of data, scenarios, and stories of how people live together in non-monogamous households. This information is sorely needed. Not only does she offer several of people's actual stories that show what it can look like to live together in a polyamorous dynamic, she also shares a lot of guidance on what works well, what has been hard, and the particular joys and pitfalls of living in this way.

In recent years, I've seen more and more people showing up to my coaching practice, following me on social media, listening to my podcast, reaching out to me for guidance, curious about polyamory. Some of that may just be that the stigma is slowly fading away and polyamory is becoming more mainstream. I also suspect though that there is a dissatisfaction with monogamy and the nuclear family unit. With housing and cost of living in general rising, home purchase increasingly out of reach for young people in the United States, most families needing two incomes to make ends meet, and the insane cost of childcare, people are increasingly creating ways to address these challenges. Not only polyamory—some people are buying homes with friends or living with extended family or building tiny house communities.

But so many of us are stuck making it up as we go along. Doing something different presents different challenges, and the solutions aren't obvious. And of course when things do go sideways, often the response from the mainstream is "This is why polyamory just doesn't work." What is often ignored is that the monogamous nuclear family is familiar, we have lots of examples of how it works, and lots of how-to books dating back through the ages. And still at least half the time, things still go sideways, and the response isn't "This is why monogamy just doesn't work."

A recurring question I get from my clients of course is "How do we do this right? How do we make this work?" Of course the answer is different for everyone, and my process of guiding them is unique to their needs and hopes. However, people who want something different than the status quo also need real examples of how it can work. They also need something they can hand the skeptics to show them, "Hey this actually is a thing people do and here's how it can work, even be great."

For too long, the available resources on polyamorous households have been minuscule. I'm so grateful that Laura has written this book—it is so needed. It's a welcome and valuable addition to the growing library of resources that can support people who are looking for how to live and love outside of the monogamous nuclear family box.

Libby Sinback
Coach, educator, mom
Host of the Making Polyamory Work podcast

CHAPTER ONE

Introduction

What is polyamory?

The term polyamory comes from the Greek *poly*, many, and the Latin *amor*, love. It's the kind of non-monogamous relationship that allows for multiple loving connections, with the knowledge of all people involved. It generally implies that all parties involved are allowed to seek additional partners, regardless of their gender, unlike the common use of the term polygamy. The term was first used in print in 1991, in an article by Morning Glory Zell-Ravenheart, and gained popularity as an alternative to the term polyfidelity, which had been previously in use within the non-monogamous community. Polyfidelity is still used by polyamorists who negotiate closing their relationships to new members today.

Throughout this book, I will use "polyamory" and "polyamorous" as baseline terms to describe the relationship style and status of the people I am discussing. Polyamory already covers a great variety of styles of relating—many of which are excluded by this book's focus on the nesting polyamorous unit—but there are still other forms of consensual non-monogamy which I am further excluding here. In practice, a relationship anarchist could use the information contained herein to build a household, but they'd do so by choosing to build a polyamorous relationship, so rather than use the expansive "non-monogamous" and then have to specify all the caveats of whom I do not mean, I will begin at "polyamorous."

There is a detailed glossary of polyamorous terms at the end of this book—it is not my intention to speak pure jargon at you at any point, but if you are jumping from chapter to chapter to find a particular issue, you may miss my definition of a particular term.

Who is polyamorous?

Everyone.

Well, about 5% of everyone.

Studies show that within North America, the only demographic along which one can predict a propensity to non-monogamy is age—and it's not exactly age, it's that Gen X and Baby Boomers have a lower percent of non-monogamy than Millennials and Gen Z. Race, education, whether you live in a city or a suburb, a "blue" or "red" area of the USA, had no significant impact on your likelihood to have been part of a non-monogamous relationship (Haupert *et al.* 2017). About 21% of adults have tried non-monogamous relationships, and between 4% and 5% identify as currently part of one. A 2023 YouGov survey confirms the overall number (6% identify as "completely non-monogamous") and breaks it down along the generational lines I laid out above (Sanders 2023).

A good chunk of these polyamorous folk have kids, and cohabit. It's harder to gather good data on this, because polyamory is not a protected status and so folks are less willing to share details of their relationships and private lives. Folks who do not live in homes with more than three adults often use the appearance of living in a "normal" couple to allow them the legal and structural privileges that come from doing so. These include things like not running afoul of zoning rules or of landlords who only want to rent to a traditional family; as well as the over 1100 federal laws that come into effect upon marriage in the US, many of which affect inheritance, taxation, and health benefits. Legal advocacy for polyamorous families in the US, which will come up as it affects the households we talk about in chapters 8, 9, 10, and 11, has been focused on the most visible of these rights: health insurance, child custody, renters' rights, and inheritance.

Part of the process of normalizing non-monogamy and polyamory in the public eye has been repeated media profiles of folks who live in household groups of three or four. This has, honestly, become a stereotype that the polyamorous and broader consensually non-monogamous community decries ("We aren't all throuples who nest" is a TikTok I've made, and I'm not the only one, by a long shot), but these families are the first public face of non-monogamy that many monogamous folks encounter.

The polyamorous family

As noted, not everyone lives in households with their partners, their metamours (partner's partners), or some combination—but as I'm going to explain in more detail below, these are the families I focus on in this book. There are plenty of social scripts for living as a couple, or a family built out of a dyad with kids. Increasingly, there are good resources for step-parenting, for blended families of remarried monogamous parents, but when there are more than two parents involved and there are affective bonds—when parents are emotionally, sexually, or intimately involved—there are no resources, there are no social scripts, and the reaction folks get can be very negative. A significant portion of my coaching practice is about helping folks navigate combining households, both internally (among themselves and with children if they have any) and externally (with family and friends, especially monogamous friends).

There is enormous variety in polyamorous households—including whether they like the term "polyamorous family" to describe themselves—and I have done my best to try to represent some of this variety and give you options and scripts to take with you into the future of your non-monogamy, whether you choose to follow them or not.

The survey

When I decided to open up a survey about polyamorous households, I asked myself how I'd keep the scope narrow enough to make the information intelligible enough that I, as someone whose education isn't in sciences, could follow it to useful conclusions. I decided to narrow my survey to folks who were, or had been, in households of three or more adults. This necessarily excludes an enormous portion of the non-monogamous community, who live alone or in a dyad and relate non-monogamously with more people. However, to address those dynamics would take a great deal more attention and complication than my simple survey and its follow-up interviewing had available. To encourage participation, I made a very simple ten-question survey, the last question of which was whether folks would be willing to do more detailed follow-up. I got 468 responses to the simple survey; 162 detailed responses of some kind, mostly a willingness to give longer-form answers by email about how their households work or had changed over time; and I conducted phone and Zoom interviews with 128 of those 162 people who were more willing to do follow-up. With their consent, some of those stories appear in this book. All names used are pseudonyms. I include an appendix tracking which households and families I reference in which chapters at the end of the book for your reference, in case it gets confusing or you think you recognize a name from a prior chapter.

I am based in the United States and so is the vast majority of my audience over social media, from which the bulk of my survey respondents came. A few live in England, a few in Australia, a few in Canada, and one in New Zealand, by self-disclosure. It is possible there is some additional variation that folks chose not to disclose, because it would have required agreeing to follow-up questions. I am comfortable using the data available on percentage of the population engaging in consensual non-monogamies from US- and Canada-based studies, therefore, as broadly representative for the populations from which I drew my survey respondents. The repeated studies (Matsick *et al.* 2014; Rubel and Bogaert 2015; Rubin *et al.* 2014) that show that in the US and Canada about 20% of adults engage in non-monogamous relationships at some point in their lives and between 4% and 5% are presently engaged in non-monogamous relationships (about 10 million adults) seem to be consistent with recent polls (Sanders 2023) indicating that 6% of adults are in "completely non-monogamous" relationships. These numbers may be gradually increasing over time, as that 1% increase suggests, and as the much higher number of Gen Z and Millennial folks who identify themselves as either in or willing to engage in non-monogamous relationships compared to Gen X and Baby Boomer folks doing the same suggests. However, more research is needed to confirm this apparent increase.

Polyamorous folk choosing to reside in groups is not a new phenomenon. The willingness of folks to self-disclose and be part of studies appears to be increasing as, despite cultural polarization and the continued lack of protected status for relationship style (only three cities in the United States—Somerville and Cambridge, MA, and Berkeley, CA—have passed non-discrimination laws based on family structure as of early 2024), polyamory enters mainstream discussion more often. Of my respondents, over half (58%) were "out" about their polyamory in some capacity.

Some considerations

As I noted above, people engage in polyamory in a variety of ways, and this book cannot be comprehensive of all of them. I do my best to deal with the major themes I uncovered and confirmed through these surveys and interviews. I say "and confirmed," because as someone who previously lived in a polyamorous household, who is polyamorous, and who has many friends and partners who currently live in some configuration of multiple adults, I had some thoughts about the variety of ways these households tend to look, some of which were confirmed by my survey and some of which were not.

I also do my best to address the common reactions to and detractors of polyamorous relationships and households. Some folks might ask, why bother with this negativity? But in the real world most polyamorous folk don't get to operate in a bubble where we only deal with other polyamorous folks, and so looking at the ways to respond to the most common criticisms can help prepare those who are considering cohabiting in a group or coparenting in a group to make an informed choice about that. There are decided benefits to non-nuclear, more-than-two-parent family choices, but there are also stigmas and complications, and I do not want to present the situation in an idealized, sunshine-and-rainbows manner. I hope that by addressing these arguments in this book, I give you some ammunition to help tell your personal critics to go jump; and that you get a bit of a laugh out of some of the chapter titles being named after common intrusive questions and comments we tend to get.

This book is not a "how to," nor does it advocate a particular "true way" of cohabitation or parenting that is superior to others. It is intended to show you a variety of ways that people choose to organize their lives and work around common issues, so that you can select the ones that make the most sense for your life. Sometimes, that may be none of them. It's absolutely a valid choice to decide that combining homes with more than one partner is a level of complicated that isn't worth it to you, regardless of the love you have for each of your partners. Having lived with partners, with a combination of partners and roommates, and with a partner and a metamour while my children were very small, I am pretty secure in my current choice to not live with any partners or metamours until my children are grown and out of my house. But I learned a lot out of those years of experience, and I would not choose otherwise than to do it if I were to start over.

There is an amazing variety of ways that people accommodate the different circumstances in their lives, only some of which are particular to polyamory, and having some of them in our back pockets as a resource to refer to can only do good for giving us scripts in a world where we have fewer. (Some might argue, none.) If the script we are selecting is a rejection of the "first comes love, then comes marriage, then comes a baby in the baby carriage" relationship escalator of monogamy, we may or may not want new ones.

I keep the concerns for children largely contained to the chapters on parenting, so that folks who are child-free but still interested in polyamorous cohabitation (over 50% of my respondents) can more easily scan those sections quickly. For those of us who are parents, and feel like the kids are woven into most areas of our lives (they are), I try to flag the places that I'm hearkening back to in the coparenting chapters—because adding kids to the mix does affect, say, picking how big a house you'll all live in or how much space adults will then have for themselves.

Why include breakups?

The breakdown of relationships, and people's understanding of their power to exit cohabiting, coparenting, or otherwise entangled relationships, is really important. The logistics of these relationships are extremely complex and often imbalanced, even in monogamous relationships. Being polyamorous does not wave a magic wand that makes us egalitarian by thought process or simplify the situation—sometimes, it adds complexity for all parties, and sometimes for only one. I am a big believer in planning for the worst and living for the best, and breakups are no exception to this.

The most common statements

The most frequently repeated statement, in emails from folks who answered follow-up questions, and on the phone, was *Well, it [is/was] just simpler*. And the second most commonly repeated statement (one I anticipated more, as we hear it and use it all the time in polyamorous circles) is *It's what works for us*. Sometimes, the latter would be the reaction to my asking questions about the former, on the phone, because "it's just simpler," applied to a schedule involving four adults and three kids, is not always easy-to-follow logic. While writing this book, I followed up with polls on my social media asking folks about these phrases—and "it's simpler" is a synonym of "given logistics have bound us into this." This book is to show you the options that exist among other people's choices—their interpretations of what was and is simpler with the same logistics of three+ adult families—so that if you decide to take them on, you don't feel quite so bound into one set of "simple" choices, and get to move into what really does work best for you, as with so much else in polyamory.

Who am I?

I've given little nods to my own polyamorous experience and previous polyamorous cohabitation and coparenting, above, but in case you wanted it directly rather than obliquely: I'm a polyamorous activist, educator, and coach who has been in non-monogamous relationships for 17 years, including some that involved cohabiting and coparenting. I'm a mom of two great kids, one of whom came home from preschool (aged three) to very solemnly inform us that most of the other kids only had one mom and that was sad. (We realized we might have a few too many polyamorous and queer friends at that point.) I had a pretty protracted de-escalation and breakup with my coparents a few years ago, and we coparent way better than we partnered or broke up, but there were a lot of lessons there. I have built a large and caring local polyamorous community here in Connecticut which is very supportive; it includes a bunch of folks who are nested in groups like the ones we're talking about, as well as a lot of dyads and solo polyamorous folks.

A large part of my coaching practice is helping people work through transitions in their relational and family life—like moving in with additional partners, the birth of children and big changes in children's lives, and breakups, which are the subjects of this book.

CHAPTER TWO

Living Arrangements and Household Dynamics

The Power of Three

The biggest question for most people is "Who will live with you?" And the next is "Where will you live?" So I opened my very simple survey with questions about these issues.

It is relatively unsurprising that the majority of family dynamics that include more than two adults include only three adults, simply because these are the next least complex structure available. Three sets of opinions, people to take into consideration, and sources of concern to worry about are easier than four or five. In the survey, 61% of my respondents live (or lived) in three-person households. Whether the three people are a triad or a vee relationship, three folks living together often saves money over a dyad doing so in terms of incomes to bills ratio, and by the time folks decide to move in they're usually fairly secure in their relationships with one another. Because not everyone who answered the survey answered follow-up questions, I don't have perfect breakdown of how many of those three-person households are triads, but of the ones who answered follow-ups, 68% are triads—so that implies that 41.5% of all respondents are nesting triads.

However, unlike folks' comments to me as I was conducting my survey about the tendency of online self-report surveys to trend the privileged and well-financed, the percentage of folks who own their homes who responded to my survey was lower than the average in both the USA and Canada, which in the US hovers around 65% and in Canada between 66% and 67%. Less than half of the people who responded to my survey own the home in which they reside—43% of respondents—and the reason is unclear. It could be because adding additional partners to the home means lots of folks are renting for a few years while they determine the needs of their expanded families (as a few follow-up interviews indicated) and figure out whether they want to all buy together; or because leases are a different kind of commitment, and previously purchased homes might not always accommodate extra adults as well; or because the studies that show that we non-monogamists really are from all over the socio-economic map are more correct than the stereotype that we're all pretty well-off. Additional study is needed to determine which of these is the most likely explanation for this surprising result.

With those caveats out of the way...

Who will live with you? And where?

For folks who come into polyamory and end up in an established, committed triad or vee relationship, moving in together can be an obvious extension of the monogamous relationship escalator. It's a clear marker of commitment, it can save money on household bills, and you might be sleeping at each other's houses a lot anyway, so someone will save on rent or mortgage payments and be able to contribute them back to other household costs. So in the same way that after several months or a year and a bit you might have a talk about moving in with a monogamous partner (Look! It's me showing my biases about timelines!), you might do it with a triad partner, or a second partner in a relationship where you're the hinge.

In that latter case, there are usually more concerns to work out. Your two partners have to get along. They have to want to live together and to spend time together well, and ideally they live in compatible ways—it's not just that you can accommodate to both their styles. (Moving in together works less well when a hinge can accommodate to both partners but the two metamours are at opposing ends of a housekeeping spectrum.) We'll talk in detail about this in Chapter 6, about sharing space with metamours (our partners' partners); but at a baseline, a whole household has to want to be a household, or have a lot of duplicated spaces.

Three is the most common number of adults to end up living together beyond two, in our couple-centric world, because even two often come from differing backgrounds where compromises need to happen in order to keep comfort and peace in the home, and odds against that get smaller with every person you add.

Zoning

Three people are the least likely to run afoul of zoning issues. While we're now living at a time where municipalities are beginning to question whether or not they should be maintaining single-family zoning as a policy, it remains in force in most cities and towns, with a variety of terms and regulations. The definition of "a family" as a legal term in different shapes for the purpose of housing is historically racist and classist (which is why it's under question or being repealed in some cities currently), so these laws are most often being enforced against folks who are marginalized in some additional way, or who are trying to live in "the good neighborhood" in a way the neighbors find disruptive. Most single-family zoning laws include a variety of ways for adults in the household to be related (blood, adoption, marriage, custodianship, or guardianship) so as not to force children or grandparents to immediately move out of a house, but they either allow none or not more than one additional unrelated adult in the household. Jurisdictions for zoning range anywhere from a municipality to a county or state that has an overriding law, so it's impossible to be comprehensive of every possibility, but broadly the trend is for families to be defined as no more than two unrelated adults residing in a house, with children; some jurisdictions additionally include a maximum number of adults per home.

Single-family zoning proliferated in the United States in the 1920s, and the combination of regulations on use and lot size have created situations where folks can't afford housing and new housing stock can't be built in a reasonable way. In California they've responded by striking down the option to create single-family zoning, but that just removes enforcement, which wasn't horribly common except by builders to begin with. But single-family zoning was adopted in the early 20th century with a rosy view of the nuclear family and how well living in one goes—and there's a lot of nostalgia for that inherent in the cultural zeitgeist at the moment. The bulk of North Americans live in single-family homes, and this is true of my respondents, too: 74% live in single-family homes whether or not they fit their local definition of a family.

In March 2015, the city of Hartford, CT brought a suit under its zoning statutes against a family group, who became known in news coverage as the "Scarborough 11" because neighbors filed complaints that their household didn't fit the definition of a single family for zoning purposes. The eight adults and three children eventually won the right to continue living in their home (a mansion in the West End of the city, definitely large enough to hold all these inhabitants)—but not until after they countersued the city, resulting in a 2017 rewrite of Hartford's zoning ordinances so as not to include parking maximums, since the number of cars was the principal complaint of neighbors. For many, a nine-bedroom house maintained with chosen family sounds like a dream. This family discovered that neighbors could decide that the adults having too many cars in the driveway was a violation of single-family zoning and make it a governmental issue, which led to years of complications.

So for some polyamorists, keeping your household smaller is a defense against potential zoning complications—"There's only one unrelated adult here!" a vee or triad that includes a married couple can say. That is not to say this is a foolproof solution to this, or that there aren't other potential issues than zoning for nesting partners seeking housing, but it's one of the considerations that seems to factor in to keeping households smaller.

Outside the US, zoning itself isn't the primary concern—single-family zoning is our own endemic problem. While parts of Canada had adopted the system, it was largely abandoned in following a 1979 legal case (*Bell* v. *The Queen*) that stated that municipalities could not determine who lived in a space, only the use of a building. However, in 2009, a case regarding a condominium held not just that single-family zoning was acceptable for condominiums in Canada, but also that the definition of a single family was a "social unit consisting of parent(s) and their children, whether natural or adopted" and included "other relatives if living with the primary group." While this has extremely rarely been upheld, and almost always against students, polyamorous families in Canada would be well advised to avoid renting or buying in a condominium setting, as this has been upheld by the Supreme Court of Canada twice.

In the UK, zoning is simply not an issue, but there are still the same kinds of stigma issues that apply to polyamorous folks everywhere (discussed in the next section). In the UK, there's a pending legal change toward the idea of "no fault" evictions, which may help reduce the impact of stigma by landlords against polyamorous tenants. As this has failed to pass into law despite being proposed in 2019, it's unclear whether it will actually effect change. Once it has and data can be collected, it will be interesting to see the impact. Keeping in mind your level of interaction with your neighbors and landlords and who is how closely entwined in your day-to-day life can help you make decisions about what makes sense to disclose upfront about who will be living with you and what your relationships are.

Regardless of what country you reside in, it's important to keep in mind your level of interaction with landlords and neighbors, and how entwined different folks are in your day-to-day life, when deciding what to disclose upfront about who lives with you and what the relationships between you are.

Bias, stigma, and practical concerns for leases and mortgages

In my survey, 11% of respondents cited having had difficulty with landlords, loans, banks, or lease agreements in the process of finding homes with their polyamorous households. This seems to align with the findings of the OPEN (Organization for Polyamory and Ethical Non-monogamy) Community Survey 2022, where 4.3% of respondents agreed with the stronger language of having experienced housing discrimination. Many of my respondents would probably not rate their experiences as discrimination, but having to adjust how they described their relationships to be allowed to sign lease agreements, having only two partners on a lease or mortgage and any additional partners not being able to gain equity in a purchased home or be officially on a lease, or even "Needing to shop around extensively for an open-minded and somewhat pushy mortgage broker to help us get a bank to give us a loan we could all be on" are all things monogamous folks don't typically have to worry about that matter to polyamorous folks navigating in a mononormative world.

The good news is that this affected only 11% of my respondents! The bad news is that if you also subtract all the people where an individual or couple already owned a home and so folks moved right in (32% of respondents), that number crawls up closer to 17%; and if we remove all the folks whose answers were about "being in cities where roommates are common" or "being young so roommates are expected," and similar, it ends up being over a quarter of people (26%) who've had some kind of negative experience seeking housing while polyamorous. This isn't to say you shouldn't seek housing as a polyam person or that you should approach this with a defeatist attitude, but know where you're looking for housing and be prepared that, depending on what your other marginalizations are, it may simplify your life to apply for a lease or buy a home in a way that looks more traditional and, as one of my respondents put it "add that roommate after the fact."

This doesn't mean that polyamorous folks can't use the "young and roommates are expected" stereotypes to our advantage when they apply—or when we live in cities, use this as well. But when we're out of these demographics, planning strategically about who will be on a lease based on whose credit is best or whose job is the easiest to document—or even who is married and easiest to explain—are all very valid choices. In terms of job documentation, if one person or only some people in your household are salary employed it may be helpful to apply for leases or mortgages using their income as opposed to that of folks who work on contract or are self-employed, regardless of the actual annual income of the individuals. This is something that doesn't always occur to folks until they themselves are self-employed or contract workers, but it came up among several of my respondents and may be one of the ways that combining household finances is challenging, and that contributes to difficulties finding housing.

The OPEN Community Survey found that 58% of non-monogamous folks are "out" in some capacities outside of just their closest friends. Cohabiting with multiple polycule members is a big impetus for many to come out.

Some big pieces of advice from folks I spoke with throughout the survey, that came up time and again:

- If you're looking at places with companies as landlords, be honest about who will reside there but don't bother trying to teach about what polyamory is; it's not the same impact as if it's someone who owns one or two rental properties where you're going to have an actual relationship with them.

- If you're trying to buy a home with three or more people, a proactive realtor or mortgage broker can really smooth the process of getting a mortgage and title in all names. It is worth the effort to shop to find one who is understanding on your side.

- Building equity is a cool goal, if you're fairly sure you're all going to continue living together. The inconveniences of having to sell and divide the equity back up again, on top of the ones of de-nesting, were cited as hugely relationship damaging by the people who shared these stories. More about this in Chapter 10.

- As an expansion of that point, put a lease or sublease agreement in writing for partners who are moving in. Owing each other money or disagreeing about what you owe "because I'm not on the lease anyway and I said I was leaving and I moved" is some prime bridge-burning behavior, and being polyamorous does not make us immune from being jerks.

- Do research on the neighborhood you're moving into—even if it's just visits and drive-throughs at different times of day and the week—and get a sense of whether it has a community vibe, whether it's an insular space, and whether the demographics of your polycule are going to stick way out. You are much more likely to run into issues with neighbors if you are a group of 20-somethings moving into a sleepy and mostly mid-50s-and-up neighborhood that rolls up the sidewalk at 9pm than if you fit in or if it's a diverse area to begin with.

Making it work

Now that we've addressed a bit of where the actual building will be, how will you decide when to form your polyamorous household and that these are the folks you want to live with? As with monogamous relationships, this is heavily personal—I cannot give you a rule-book that says everything will work if you follow this formula. If you have partners who you care a great deal for and want to move in with, and they want to as well, there are a few suggestions, gleaned from my experience as a coach and the survey, that I have to offer.

Don't move in under the influence of NRE

NRE, or new relationship energy, is sometimes simplified to "the honeymoon period." It's the giddiness and excitement (some scientists believe it's a result of a chemical flood of oxytocin and vasopressin in the brain) that can be experienced as positive butterflies and urge to spend all your time with a new partner or, on the flip side, as a need for constant reassurance that they also care for you and anxiety that your strong feelings for them are reciprocated. Many people lean toward the positive in experiencing it and ignore flags of incompatibility in relationships in the weeks or months where they're bonding with partners and having these experiences of new, loving feelings. Some folks experience this for as little as a few weeks, while others say these occasionally overwhelming feelings can last for up to two years.

Polyamorous people often report these feelings lasting longer because of the intermittent nature of our non-nesting and early relationships—when you're engaging in multiple relationships, it's harder to do the monogamous full-bore thing of seeing someone with all of your spare time (because this would involve neglecting your existing relationships), so folks are less likely to "wear the shine off" or "take off the rose colored glasses" in just a few weeks. This can make it harder to wait until you're fully clear-headed in your decision-making and examining all your possible compatibilities and incompatibilities to make a choice about moving in together.

While some people find that they have great success despite moving major steps in their relationships forward under the first blush of new love (my own parents got engaged to be married just a few months after they met and were married within the year, and are together more than 35 years later), many others find that there's less stability and intentionality in choices made in this phase of relationships. Let's look at why with some examples from participants in our survey.

MAGGIE, ALEX, AND AMY

Alex and Amy had been married for a few years when they decided to open up their relationship. Their first few attempts at relationships outside of their marriage crashed and burned in various ways—bad first dates, bad third dates, guys who decided they couldn't be dumped gracefully after a couple months, girls who decided they would live HAPPILY EVER AFTER on the second date, and a variety of other problems, by their own telling—until they met Maggie. They met at a local polyam meetup, she was already in other relationships, neither she nor they were trying to have the most intense relationship of their lives on date two—but a few months in, when Maggie's landlord was going to sell the house she was living in, they all decided moving in together, despite only knowing each other a few months, was the best solution. "We thought we were immune to the problems of NRE because we hadn't started spending all our time together the first week," Amy explained to me, "but we had a very idealized vision of our relationship, and we didn't know each other that well, we just hoped we'd make it work because of love..."

They had a lot of struggles with logistical issues and realizing that their values didn't actually align that well upon moving in—nothing so major that they had to not care about one another, but also enough that they were in frequent conflict. Where Alex and Amy had already smoothed out their incongruence in learning to live together, adding a third party brought all of the conflicts back to the fore, and highlighted the differences between things they agreed on and that Maggie didn't.

As an example, when to do dishes was a struggle. Alex and Amy had come to an agreement that dishes would get done within a couple hours of a meal getting made (by bedtime after dinner, and before the next meal during the day) to keep things from piling up, but this was not initially a thing they agreed on. Alex had been a "wash a dish the minute you use it" person, or else he'd forget it was there until the sink was full and do a whole load of dishes, and Amy liked washing a day of dishes at night. So they had come to their compromise position. Maggie being a person who also didn't value clearing a sink the instant something was dirty made for immediate logistical issues, which created low-level conflicts and highlighted disagreements between the three of them in general.

This led to more arguments where folks brought up what Amy characterized as "actual values"—"how to spend money or not, and why that's important, like I want to have experiences together but think they need to be cheap or free until household responsibilities and expenses are fully covered, and that as a household this includes all our debts—and that wasn't something we ended up agreeing about" and "feeling controlled about time—because everyone had different ideas of what quality time felt like, but we all wanted to have it with each other and that added up to a LOT of time together."

In the end, this triad actually solved their relationship concerns by de-nesting but staying in the relationship—because lowering their entanglement level back to where it had been before they let these disagreements blow up too long let them keep the love in their relationships. They lived together for 15 months and had been moved out for six months when I spoke to them initially for this survey. They were still together, just not nested, when I sent a follow-up message a year later.

Let's chat about an example where moving in under the influence of NRE worked out better, next, shall we?

EVAN, MARK, AND KEISHA

In Brooklyn, in 2014, at a party thrown by some friends, Evan and Keisha met Mark and his then partner Michelle. Mark and Michelle were the "polyamorous and loud about it, but don't worry, we aren't here to steal your girl" associates of this social circle. It wasn't something Keisha and Evan had ever run into engaged in "openly and respectfully before," Keisha told me, "and I thought they were just these really magnetic, attractive people—the energy was very good." So, Keisha and Evan got to know and pretty rapidly began to date Mark and Michelle in a quad (four-person) relationship. All four of them moved in together "unofficially… like immediately—but we got a place that was big enough and actually moved furniture about six months in." The four childless-by-choice 20-somethings had all the struggles we've already discussed about moving in together, but their attitude toward them was one of "but where is the overlap?" What could they make work together, and what did they need to keep separated because of those differences in attitude, in order to keep things moving smoothly?

By adopting this attitude, and regular check-ins about what was working and what wasn't in their household, they lived pretty happily and uneventfully as a quad for five years, until Michelle and her other partner Devon decided they wanted to have kids, and Michelle moved out. This destabilized things somewhat, because de-nesting is a hard transition to manage while remaining together, and Michelle is now partnered only with Evan out of the nesting triad as it remains. The three of them—Evan, Keisha, and Mark—have remained happily together for the last four years. They have a good system for household tasks they've settled into,

> they all sometimes have date nights with partners from outside the home, and folks are surprised but find it romantic that they moved in to their two-bedroom apartment six months after they met.

So, what happens if, instead of de-nesting, more partners move in?

This was a constant (and often sarcastic) question we would get when I lived in a vee. "Is everyone just going to move in with you?" And first, this obviously doesn't make sense, because from a perspective of who fits where (which we talk about more in the next two chapters) it doesn't much work—but also because who really wants to live in the most convoluted constellation polycule house? The interpersonal dynamics at a certain point get complex.

Our world, whether we prefer this or not, is largely built for families with two adults and some kids, or at best, intergenerational living with grandparents along, or a few roommates. It is not generally constructed for the egalitarian presence in a home of four to eight adults, who may then also add some children. My polycule, at the time that people were sarcastically asking me this, was largely composed of polyam parents dating one another in a chain so it also would have required enormous space resources for the number of kids involved (and then to be in a good school system!) so it was really impractical. No matter your emotional entanglements, everyone has different practical considerations that will place limits on when, whether, and how nesting is an option for them. If nesting with all your partners eventually is a goal of yours, there are some different considerations you may have to keep in mind.

People who are striving to add more folks to their nested polycules, or who are trying to keep from putting ceilings on additional relationships, may need to date with compatibility of their partners, not just themselves, in mind. In that previous example, if the quad had as a group decided that childrearing was okay but they didn't all want to be the biological parents, Devon might have moved in with them—a different series of transitions than the ones they chose to go through in reality. Dating for personal compatibility in that case meant that Michelle got to meet Devon, move out and go form a childrearing unit while still maintaining a romantic relationship with Evan; dating with polycule compatibility in mind would have meant considering that the polycule as a whole was dedicated to a child-free home and placing that ceiling on her relationship with Devon or not forming that relationship to begin with. There is no requirement in polyamory to date with a whole polycule in mind but many people choose to—especially when they're highly logistically entangled, like nesting or having had a family with some partners.

Something that comes up in polyamorous support groups often is that no relationship is easier than others—it's a matter of choosing the "kind of hard" that's best aligned with your values and wants. As someone who wholeheartedly supports folks who are monogamous as well as those who prefer to live in various configurations of non-monogamous relationship, this has always made sense to me. It's the kind of hard that feels worth it to you—there's no such thing as a relationship that's always easy, just one that brings you the most joy and matches your philosophy best in-between the challenging moments.

Roommate compatibility

I mentioned this for a moment at the start of this chapter—that folks are often raised with very different standards for what's important in keeping house or different priorities of what matters in how a household functions. It is one thing to love someone and an entirely different one to live with them well. Do you care about the same kinds of mess? Do you have the same priority on not letting outside clothes touch the bed? Does one of you not function well in a disorganized space and the other rank tidying below a number of other life priorities like social time, work time, spending time with family, having time to themself, and more? These might be incompatibilities. Not all of them are insurmountable—we'll talk about ways that people overcome minor differences in who prioritizes which chores and things like this in later chapters—but broad strokes awareness of whom you are choosing to move in with and not expecting complete transformation is in your best interest.

So is applying the "roommate standard" to all your behavior while living with partners and metamours. If you wouldn't behave that way to a roommate, why are you treating your partner or meta that way? Your behavior should be at least as conscientious as that you'd offer a roommate. So, for example, you should ask before letting a guest or non-nesting partner use something that belongs personally to your nesting partner, whether it's their pillow or a sweater or their favorite mug. Instead you can offer the non-nesting partner one in the house that is neutral or your own, especially if you don't have a minute to ask your nesting partner first. Taking a second to pause before you move forward with a plan and think about how you'd feel if a roommate did it to you can keep conflicts on a much smaller scale.

It can also really improve communication about conflict to determine whether any issue is one you would have with a partner or meta even if it occurred without any of the other relationship situations that exist, or whether you're projecting insecurity about a non-nesting relationship onto a partner's (annoying but minor) failure to pick up socks today. Admitting what a fight is about is a great step toward resolving it in a more measured and mature way.

If you're going to live with someone who isn't your partner, test-driving roommate compatibility by trying out the arrangement with extended kitchen table time where you don't get treated like a guest can be really important. Whether that means sending the shared partner away for a day or two and having metamour-bonding time while you figure out that one of you puts the cups away upside down and it makes the other one nuts (but in a manageable way), or all spending lots of time together in each other's spaces so no one feels like they are in charge more of the time, to get a feel for one another, creating that environment to know one another well enough that it's not a big shock how you interact.

CHAPTER THREE

"But Where Do You All Sleep?"

In my coaching practice, the most common reasons folks seek me out for group or three+ person coaching (as opposed to seeing me as individuals or in dyads) is to prepare for the process of moving in together, or deal with bumps in the road of their relationships that have occurred in the process of moving in together. By the time they're determined to move in they've usually addressed the emotional concerns of relationship progress, but often the logistical concerns feel overwhelming. The external, monogamy-centered question of "But where do you all sleep?" can be a first logistical question to begin with for many households. Other questions concern personal storage space, use of bathrooms, and who does what chores.

Bedrooms

Let's take one step back—before you figure out "where you all sleep" within a space, you need some idea of the space you're working with. These two steps often flip-flop in position for households, depending on if someone owns a home that the polycule intends to live in. About 55% of my respondents for the survey of polyamorous households with three+ adults owned the home in which they reside, and 45% rented. This is partly because, as polyamory is not a protected class, landlords can refuse rentals based on membership of this group. It's also because the folks who are most comfortable being "out" and participating in a survey like mine are likely to be higher-income, older, and therefore more likely (demographically) to own their homes. The shape of a home you own may therefore limit the number of bedrooms you have to work with in determining who sleeps where in the short term—or may require you to renovate, if that's financially feasible.

If everyone is renting prior to moving in together, the choice to rent together may allow you to approach this question of "Where does everyone sleep?" (and when) as a starting point that shapes the home you choose. As an example to help you visualize thinking about this, I'd like to describe my own living situation when I lived in a V relationship. I, my partner, and my metamour were moving into a house with our infant child. There were four bedrooms, and two bathrooms, none of which were attached to a bedroom. (The 2000s and onward trend of the ensuite bathroom had not touched this 1980s construction.) Two bedrooms were larger and positioned to share one of the bathrooms, and the other two smaller and set up to share the other. We decided that all the adults would share one of the bathrooms and the two big bedrooms. I lived in one, and my meta in the other, and the hinge switched between them depending on our schedules. His stuff was spread across the two closets and he had smaller chests of drawers in both rooms. We had a "baby's room" and a "guest room" by the other bathroom to round out our use of bedrooms. Later in that relationship when he got non-nesting partners, they'd spend overnights in the guest room to not displace anyone from their room, and his computer was in there to give a little bit of private space to retreat to that didn't "belong to anyone else." There are triads and Vs that happily all share a bedroom or bed in order to give more space or more room to children or to home offices (especially in a post-2020 world), and that's an equally valid choice. It would not have worked for me, or for us, in the years we lived together. Knowing that we needed two bedrooms for the adults plus as many rooms as kids once they stopped being babies shaped our family's space requirements over time.

Solutions

What are some of these solutions polyamorous people might come up with for where they might sleep, and how?

There's the clear solution of three in one bed—a king bed for three adults is manageable for some folks, especially if they are comfortable and all involved with one another. Triads sometimes elect for this option.

For those who have a big bedroom and are all together, there can be alternative bedding options. Some folks put two beds together in order to create bigger spaces for three or more partners to share—the inexpensive option to add little bed bridges that are meant to combine two twins but instead to combine two queen beds can really improve folks' quality of life. The internet is full of recommendations for polyamorous people to remember to add extra blankets so that the person in the middle can control their own temperature and isn't overheated by the partners on either side, as well as commentary of people who want to build custom larger beds to fit greater than three groups.

However, for many, it is impractical to actually sleep all together. Just as many monogamous couples find that sleeping together every night actually lowers quality of sleep because of schedule, tossing and turning, or snoring, polyamorous folks have similar concerns. Some deal with this by putting two beds in large master bedrooms if they have the space; others have two or more bedrooms and rotate between them.

Others have individually assigned bedrooms, and either "visit" for "dates" to spend time with their partners or have hinge partners share rooms with spoke partners some or all of the time. As we mentioned earlier in this chapter, sometimes, due to space constraints, not all partners can have individual rooms and private space is at a premium; here, a partner may bounce from room to room.

Folks with young children sometimes find that prioritizing space for the parent who is the preferred sleeping companion of small children is an important choice, and that making whatever "date" or sexuality time choices they may make for a portion of evening or nighttime is a separate concern from actual overnight decisions. Children sometimes make these choices for us—it can be hard to predict how often or for how many years we'll have nocturnal visitors, and going with the flow can be the most important skill parents and their nesting partners acquire.

What about non-nesting partners?

The biggest tradeoff I hear people describe in talking to me about their space requirements is whether they will maintain individual bedrooms for adults or generally shared bedrooms and "a guest room" for visiting non-nesting partners. As we've discussed previously, while three adults is the most common size of household, it is not the most common size of polycule—most of these relationships remain open, or involve additional members who do not reside in the household, and folks have to agree about how they handle that.

Younger people, of the Millennial or Gen Z cohorts, have generally had extended experience with roommates (cue the "Monogamy? In this economy?" jokes) and so have expectations around how they intend to handle sexy visitors. Some folks have emotional trouble decoupling their partnership with folks from their reaction and so adjust their expectations and agreements accordingly—they'll go out on their partner's date nights and have a quiet hour, for example—and some folks had those agreements to be polite roommates anyway and consider it par for the course. Communication is at the heart of those issues.

For some, especially for those with kids who are using every room in their home or those in urban areas where rent is prohibitive so room sharing is essential to keeping their space, agreements about when bringing non-nesting partners over is OK look different and involve not having sleepovers unless the nesting partner is out for their own sleepover at someone else's home or out of town for work, for example. This is a situation where everyone's individual requirements differ and we can't apply judgment about how we would do things to someone else's choices about how they choose to do things.

Some examples of ways folks might handle incorporating space for non-nesting partners and their dates into home choices:

- if you have enough money, a guest room folks can use when they bring non-nesting partners home (especially helpful if one or more partners find their bed to be "private space")

- separate bedrooms for all partners and "visiting" each other in one another's rooms for sleepovers on date days/nights, so any non-nesting partners visit just like nesting partners do (great for non-hierarchical polycules)

- a pull-out couch that one person can crash on if bedroom spaces need re-assigning because of guests (it can either be for a non-nesting partner after a date, or for a nesting partner who's giving up their bed to be kind)

- putting that pull-out couch or convertible bed into a home office, so that whoever's office it is has personal space even if they aren't bringing a partner home (good for when folks are sharing space all the time).

Deciding among parenting partners (with input from the affected parties!) how to handle if non-parenting partners are over when kids climb in bed can be important—will the partner be banished to couches? Is Mom or Dad going to get out and go put Kiddo back in their own bed? (Will Mom or Dad end up asleep balanced on the edge of a twin bed or on the floor next to it, holding a small hand?) Is there an age at which your answers change? Do you just prefer that partners wear pajamas in the house when kids are there and otherwise you don't have big opinions? Get on the same page. If the affected partner is *less* comfortable than you are, their comfort rules. If they'd be okay to interact with kids, your rules preside.

In summary for bedrooms

Bedrooms often define how people determine what kind of space they're going to buy or rent. What you can afford in your area can shift your use-case a lot—people in really pricy areas who are trying to save money might be more willing to sleep more to one room on an everyday basis, and have a guest room all partners share for "date night" retreats, whether that's with nesting or non-nesting partners. People who are less willing to share a room, and need private space, might be more willing to share bathrooms or public spaces or "date night" space with other folks who live in the household.

Beds? What about closet space?

The same considerations that drive monogamous couples to

pick spaces can drive polyamorous folks when making their choices in selecting a home to reside in together—or in selecting which rooms to use for whom in a house. Who has the most clothes? How will you store them? Are there enough closets? An older home that lacks closets but has enough room for standing storage like wardrobes and dressers can make some choices simpler, and others more difficult.

In conducting my survey I spoke with Eva, a member of an East Coast lesbian triad who had inherited a house from an elderly grandparent. The hundred-year-old house they moved into had great character, especially in public rooms of the home, but almost no storage built in within the bedrooms. "We had a vision of each having our own room with big beds and our clothes separated out," she explained to me, "but as we started cleaning things up and taking measurements to move in, we realized if we wanted larger beds, we weren't going to be able to open armoires and dressers on either side, and it got impractical really fast." The triad ended up deciding to have a shared everyday bedroom, a guest room to which they could retreat if they wanted private time, and a "dressing room" that they decorated for relaxing and filled with their clothes, mirrors, and a long, low couch. "It's like the ultimate walk-in closet," she told me with a laugh.

Many folks do smaller versions of this, without redecorating entire rooms as shared walk-ins, by doing things like moving a dresser to a home office space, or placing an armoire in a guest room. This is certainly not unique to polyamorous individuals, but if three people are attempting to share closet space meant for one or for two at the most, it becomes more likely that creative solutions will need to be found.

Closets and storage are also a significant part of many folks' choices around how to keep sound from traveling excessively within their homes. Many people I spoke with in follow-up interviews mentioned choices like putting wardrobes and bookshelves on adjoining walls when there weren't closets between bedrooms, to do some sound dampening between rooms.

Folks who own their homes sometimes do remodels, either minor or major, to allow for better or more usable closet space—if rooms are large, building a wall out so that closets are built-in rather than furniture pieces, or if they're smaller but there's room to be taken from other spaces in the house, doing the same from other rooms.

Bathrooms

In addition to all of these concerns about bedrooms and closets, we then hit the issue of bathrooms. That's the one that's less often asked about by strangers, friends, or family, but more often a concern when folks are picking out a home, or a point of conflict after having done so.

Different people and families have very different priorities when it comes to bathrooms. I mentioned before when I lived with my now-coparents and kids. Our priority was that the tubs be good for giving our babies baths and that none of the bathrooms be shut into one of the bedrooms so that it was inaccessible without crossing someone's private space. That latter point—that the now-popular ensuite master bath may not suit a polyamorous household as well as a monogamous one, unless it's a triad who all share the master bedroom and bath—is a common concern. The style of bathroom folks prefer will be more personal, and the 1980s narrow step-in tubs of our house may be exactly what someone doesn't want. A person or family with physical disabilities or mobility concerns may prioritize a shower they can walk into in at least one bathroom, for example.

One family I spoke with, from Portland, Oregon, moved into their home as a triad with young kids, and were very pleased with the set-up of one very fancy bathroom ensuite to the master bedroom, one more basic one on the hallway, and a half-bath for guests off the kitchen; but a few years into living together, there was a breakup between two of the three adults in the family and they stopped all sharing that master bedroom. Now that Amanda, who I principally interviewed, was living in her own room, and sharing the hallway bath with the kids, things felt unbalanced as opposed to when all the adults had easy access to the bathroom with a soaking tub and nicer finishes. Her ex, Susan, and their shared partner, Ben, both agreed that she could use that bathroom when she wanted, but having to go through her ex's bedroom to use it made it an awkward transition for her, and something that she only wanted to do if no one was home, or in really private time, which was in relatively short supply. It was a serious mental transition. The three of them were in the middle of getting quotes for putting in a door from the hallway into the bathroom directly, since the plumbing was not in the way of doing so.

Changes like that—putting in extra doors to make the "fancy bath" accessible to more than one bedroom, or renovating a hallway bathroom to be the updated bathroom rather than the ensuite one—are choices that run counter to standard real estate agent advice for reselling a home but that can make a home more useful for a polycule. Standard advice tends to assume that no more than two adults will be living in a home, and that finishes on spaces for guests or for children can be managed later or at a lesser level—but when there are three, four or five of you all sharing a property as equals, the choices are different.

Chores

The household logistical question that is not asked by outsiders, but is often recognized by those inside relationships (and occasionally acknowledged by think-pieces about the mental load of household tasks) is "Who will do all the chores of a house with more people in it?" While the truism "many hands make light work" can apply here, the idea that "someone else will do it so why should I" can keep anyone from getting started on many tasks. This is a subject where it is hard to give advice, because different households will find different approaches to be functional, reasonable, and equitable for them. That last point is the one essential piece of advice I can offer—equity, not equality, is the goal in the division of household labor.

What is equity in labor?

Equity rather than equality means we are not going to make a list of 18 tasks that need doing by three adults, give each of you six, and say that this is perfect. Equity means considering that some of these are bigger tasks than others; that some of them are tasks one person finds easier, relaxing, or meditative, while another finds them odious; and that someone went around and made the list in the first place, which is a 19th task and not a small one, often.

There are techniques for dividing household labor that are growing in popularity, like habit-building apps or chore-gamifying apps that let you "build a party" to do your chores with, or Fair Play cards that let you divide and redivide tasks in different ways until you find a system you feel is equitable. However, most commonly, folks trial and error things until they find a system that works for their household.

Having honest conversations before you move in together about what chores folks dislike the most, avoid the most, are most likely to default to doing (whether because they, for example, hate seeing dishes in the sink, or because they actually like doing dishes), or ones they are happier to do than others is really important. If it turns out you're all people who are really content to do dishes, but no one is a laundry person, figure out a schedule to rotate it. If you each have a different thing you default to, great, each of you has a first job that's yours, and you can take the temperature of why people default to it; and if it's a positive reason, then you can proceed neutrally to assigning more tasks; and if it's because it not being done makes living in a space harder or uncomfortable for the person who does it (or because of resentment and frustration that it isn't done), you can give that person the choice of a positive chore on the next round. Proceed with positive and neutral chores until there aren't any left and you've got only chores people really don't like left.

You also get to decide among yourselves, through honest analysis of time spent in the home versus at work and commuting, whether there is someone who is at home more who might do more chores, and if so whether there is something other folks can do to balance that extra work they're doing. Housework is still labor, even if it's discounted compared to labor outside the home. It may be more convenient for the person who works from home to do and fold laundry between meetings, for example—but they are still working so it can go either way whether they pick up more chores.

I know these are also concerns in monogamous households, but polyamorous folks often fall into the trap of assuming that because there are more people, these things will automatically be resolved more easily. And we need to consider that polyamorous folks frequently plan more social time both in and out of the home that eats into the time that we usually use and need to complete household tasks.

Assumptions and gender roles

As in so much of polyamory, there are assumptions and norms that can be taken apart here that improve folks' odds of success as a household in the long term. I spoke with John, a member of a large polyamorous household in Massachusetts that includes five networked relationship members and one roommate who was not in an intimate relationship with the other folks in the household, about their eight years (and counting) living together.

"The first couple years were rocky," he told me, "in large part because we kind of expected my wife and her girlfriend to always tell us what needed doing, and then we 'would help' with the housework. Over time we realized that wasn't sustainable and figured out systems to take charge of chores we generally were doing anyway and stopped doing the social 'dumb man' routine. There's a lot of conditioning to wait until you're told about anything, but it was the yard that I, Josh, Dave and Mark [the other household members] all had to get over to make things work without making things unfair and the women at home go crazy."

This was the most explicit statement of one trend I heard while asking throughout follow-up interviews what advice people had for cohabitation—that if there is someone or someones who tend to carry extra weight or mental load in planning, whether it be scheduling for a family or household, or chores, or being in charge of kin-keeping, that weight has to be let up somewhere. So if the person carrying this mental load and doing the assignment of tasks is doing many fewer of them and is in fact, mostly just the manager of your household and double-checking that things get done—great! But if they're doing that *and* doing a similar number of the tasks as everyone else? There's a chance for some resentment to form and foment there. That's something that should be checked in on or mitigated. If they want to take that on, it's okay, but as a household work together on learning to actually let go of delegated tasks so that, for example, no one is going behind anyone else saying *how* a towel should be folded if towels are in fact, folded and on a correct shelf or in a correct drawer. This is a team effort, to release some of this load not only by learning to take ownership of tasks, knowing how often one does them, and anticipating them instead of needing constant reminders (like so much else in polyamory, a calendar alert can be a friend for that), but also by learning to let the person who does a task just do it. Done is enough.

It is most often, but not always, women who have these roles of having the mental load and a set of expectations of what needs doing when and men who act as though they can't see mess around them until told it needs dealing with. This is by no means universal, however, and as with everything else, unpack and address what needs unpacking within your own relationships and household. The real fundamental point is to work together on it. If you leave it to be one person's problem, or to be "We'll all help when you schedule Cleaning Day in the calendar and until then you've got it, right?" it's much easier to hit a place where folks feel unheard, unappreciated, and like they're the only ones putting in effort.

Schedules

In monogamy (and in roommate-land, where many of us get our expectations about household chores if they differ from those we were raised with) we might have the expectation that there can be a "Cleaning Day" we set aside to do these things together. In a polyamorous household and schedule, a common complaint I heard was that doing this meant that you lost a day with your nesting partners in favor of completing this, while non-nesting folks lose nothing, or that more interesting plans with folks who aren't nested win out and the household goes uncared for until it hits a point of desperation when everyone kicks in effort. This can feed back into that loop we mentioned above where it becomes one person's job to notice the problems and enlist others, delegating tasks to them. It's not a uniquely polyam problem to be busy, but polyamorous people take overscheduling to the next level sometimes. The advice to take time for yourself can sometimes get subsumed into the necessary time to do household care tasks, especially if folks are in a season of dating a lot or early in a relationship and spending a lot of time outside a home—and this can be more common than people expect, because not everyone experiences it at once. "Spontaneity" or the illusion thereof can also be more challenging for folks who are trying to balance many people's needs.

Ethan, from Chicago, who lives with his partners Jennifer and Melissa, shared with me some of their recent struggles with household management:

> Our biggest challenge in moving in together has been hitting our stride in cleaning and organizing. We didn't expect that, because we all kept similarly clean apartments alone (or with other roommates). Somehow, all living together everyone else's mess was in the way every time one of us wanted to bring an external date over, but none of us wanted to step on toes by clearing all of someone's things out of the common areas—like the girls moving a puzzle I was building into my room, for example—without the other there, and we were rarely home at once unless it was mutual date time. Who wants to clean during date time? So it took some time and deliberate scheduling to figure out systems of asking and signaling what's okay to move and also scheduling in some shared cleaning separate from dates.

When I followed up with him, I learned that the three of them, although they had similar standards of cleanliness in general, had very different standards for guests and for people new to their home, and had run into conflict around that specifically. Where Jennifer would hear that any of them was planning to bring a new date home for the first time and she'd want to clean the entire house to make a good impression of their (her) housekeeping, the others considered their baseline basically fine at all times, even with new people. These differing standards that they hadn't thought to discuss until they became a recurring small conflict were solved by relatively simple systems—agreeing that it was okay to put things away into private spaces where guests wouldn't see them unless specifically marked, and trying to contain things like big art projects into specific designated areas so they didn't overrun the home—but it hadn't occurred to Melissa and Ethan that if they thought the house was alright, they might still have to tidy a little extra so that everyone was comfortable with non-residents seeing it.

The timing of doing this can be likewise challenging—if everyone is trying to make dates with folks outside the home and doing calendaring independently with partners who have their own limitations, and trying to make sure the relationships within the home (in this case, a triad of Ethan, Jennifer, and Melissa and the dyads within that) all have time to connect there can be a fair amount of scheduling stress. Spontaneity can be a beautiful ideal but one that requires a fair amount of remembering to ask for what you need, consistently.

CHAPTER FOUR

"I Could Never Do That"

Challenging preconceptions

One of the deep stereotypes of polyamory (one that is absolutely based in reality) is the number of people who will hear that you are polyamorous and immediately respond with "I could never do that" as if you had asked them to. The existence of your relationships is treated as an attack on their relationships or their wishes for monogamous relationships. In many ways, the best way to counteract the force of "I could never do that" is to remind folks they aren't being asked to; and from another angle, the best way to counteract this cultural force is to zoom out and look at where it comes from. So let's look at the cultural and personal frameworks of relationships that people are tapping into when they hit you with "I could never do that" and how those impact our actual relationships and the way we live them in polyamorous households.

In order to approach this we need to talk about what monogamy *is*, culturally. Monogamy sits on more than one pillar. Yes, exclusivity is the major pillar that folks think of that is the first issue. But exclusivity is just one of the pillars on which monogamy and couplehood, the social construct, sits. Another is this idea that the couple and the romantic relationship sits at the top of a social hierarchy—that your romances are or should be more important than your family and both should be more important than friendships. A third is the idea that your romantic partner should be your everything, your soulmate, your best friend, your roommate and coparent and the only one to whom you're attracted.

Polyamory has the possibility to undercut all of these, not just the question of exclusivity, and cohabiting while polyamorous generally does undercut many of these. We do not have to make every one of our relationships off the relationship escalator and non-traditional in order to understand that our relationships don't have to be all things to us; and we can decide where we want our relationships to sit in our personal social hierarchy—Is romance king? Is family number one? Do we prioritize chosen family that includes our romantic partners? There are choices available. We get to have a more expansive framework when we move outside monogamy. But questioning this hierarchy of the importance of the romantic relationship is actually the thing that monogamous people are usually the most upset by when they say "I could never do that"—they mean "Why are you questioning my priorities?"

I'm not objecting to someone else prioritizing their romantic partner above other obligations, I'm saying that when someone asks me how I could possibly decide if both my romantic partners had an emergency at once, I hear nonsense, because both my partners have large support networks and don't solely rely on me. So yes, I would do my best to triage and support, but also they'd both have a team.

This feeds into cultural questions about what a family is. We're living in a moment of huge expansion of understanding about this. My son was three and in pre-kindergarten several years ago having a discussion about "all kinds of families" that included single-parent, divorced households with up to four parents, and two parents of different gender combinations, when I realized how much the conversation had moved forward from when I was a child. Polyamorous families do sometimes move this even further, as chosen families that do or don't involve kids but involve a lot of affective bonds.

Dr. Elisabeth Sheff coined a term for all the relationships that exist as a side effect of our polyamorous relationships—she calls them *polyaffective relationships,* and this term includes everything from "bonus grandparents" our children gain when we live with partners who become like parents to them, to close friendships with our metamours, and more. These non-marital and non-biological parental bonds between live-in partners and children are deep according to her 20-year longitudinal study of polyamorous families, and all the polyaffective bonds can help hold families together. In Sheff's study, these relationships between metamours, and between kids and parents' partners are a great predictor of the health of households and polycules long term (Sheff 2020).

They're closer than "just friendship," classically, because one spends a great deal of time and energy being mutually supportive and building into these relationships, whether or not folks decide to move in together as the folks who took part in my study have done with at least some of their polycule. This sits in connection to the gay community's concept of "chosen family," which has spread via many scholars and social references into the mainstream—the idea that we can rely on supportive relationships that aren't with biological or legal family and treat them as a family, as a support network.

The metamour who shows up with food when you're in the hospital so your partner can continue supporting you; partners who tradeoff caring for an ill partner and for their kids; coparents who provide backup for moments difficult and beautiful, whether or not they're romantically entangled with you—these are all kinds of chosen family that our society is pretty quick to dismiss as less than. The social norm of monogamy is happy to grant us joy in a big support network of friends *if* we haven't found a romantic relationship to zero in on, but we're expected to put it aside for romance and the nuclear family as our number one priority. Polyamorous people can make the choice to continue prioritizing these relationships outside our romances—or to expand our families by expanding our romantic networks.

So, are chosen families our families? Are they full families? Are all the aunties and uncles who aren't related by blood, and the dozen names for additional parents we'll talk about in Chapter 8, people who together make a family for children or for themselves? Are a group of childless adults still a family if they aren't also blood-related? Our culture will generally grant that they are if they happen to include marriages or blood relationships. As we move forward in considering the challenges and strategies to overcome them that polyamorous folks often face and employ, we're going to return to this idea of building family and identifying who wants to be part of family, and how big a part, as a unifying strategy.

Problems in relationship networks

When people say "I could never do that" part of what they are imagining is that all problems polyamorous people face ripple across an entire polycule—that any interaction with your metamour means a fight that affects you, them, and your shared partner, and that all disagreements are metamour problems. In reality, most of the time, when we think we have a metamour problem, what we actually have is a partner problem. Most interpersonal issues exist between two people at once, not a whole network.

People are generally quick to give their metamours the blame for things that are their partner's issues, at least until they build individual polyaffective relationships. These relationships really are the glue that holds polycules together. The most common categories of conflict that are going on when folks think they have a metamour problem are:

1. a partner problem
2. a communication problem
3. a time-management problem
4. a partner's boundary-holding problem
5. an insecurity problem on your part
6. a rule in a previously existing relationship you weren't informed of, enforced heavily
7. hierarchy you didn't know existed (not knowing it exists is 1, 2, or both)
8. blame being passed along unfairly (1–4 with some fancy make-up on).

Numbers 6 and 7 should be resolved between folks who are going to live together before moving in, but may come up with new partners and non-nesting partners, because every relationship is unique and there are always possibilities for miscommunication of rules and details. You might run into the need to enforce a rule or a hierarchy the household had established (that children's needs come first, or nesting partnerships' needs come first) for the first time, and have thought that this was self-explanatory, because it is an extension of the monogamous paradigm where the couple and the nuclear family are at the top of a hierarchy. Folks who have been polyamorous for a while have often unpacked this and discarded this assumption, and this can cause conflict. The conflict can become phrased as "My meta won't let my partner do XYZ with me on this day" when actually it's an issue of "My partner is in this hierarchical system and didn't bother to tell me" or "My partner had agreed to a rule about when XYZ can happen and didn't tell me until she thought it was relevant, and that was after it was a surprise to me."

Realizing in the heat of feelings where to manage conflict and how to see the issue as the problem and not a partner or meta as the problem can be really challenging. Recognizing that in our instinct not to blame our partner, we don't get to deflect blame and rules and hierarchy onto our metamours is a process that many people only complete after building those polyaffective bonds we talked about above.

It's much harder to deflect and project onto someone when they're genuinely one of your closest relationships (although certainly not impossible—ask most of us who have ever been in therapy working on our own shadow selves). When people lack a connection of friendship or closeness with metamours, it's easier to hear a partner enforcing their own boundaries as a rule being imposed by a third party. In cases where there is a rule in place that's affecting you, it's much easier to address and discuss it if you aren't regarding anyone who is a party to the rule as an adversary. Let's consider an example from a family I spoke to in the survey.

JOSH, JONAH, AND DEBBIE

Jonah and Debbie had been part of a nesting quad who were co-parenting for several years when Debbie met her newer partner Josh. Debbie and Josh were dating for several months happily when their relationship ran directly into a rule the nesting relationship had in place: no trips longer than a weekend away with anyone except the nesting family. (This was partly to simplify finances, she explained, and partly a thing that made them all feel a little special or a hierarchy hangover—they weren't formally hierarchical but a couple of their rules felt a little like it.) So when Josh invited Debbie away for a week and she declined, explaining this rule, and that she couldn't go even if he covered the finances, he felt very put off, and blamed all her nesting partners. He especially blamed her husband, Jonah, she told me, because the feeling that this rule was arbitrary and that it related to their children, that it was a hangover from having been monogamous, and that the long vacation they did take was to a beach house they'd always gone to with the kids and the one change or addition they'd made was that their nesting partners could join them, sat very poorly with Josh. He felt like Jonah was the one controlling what outings and vacations he and Debbie could take, even though Debbie had agreed to it and was the one who had explained it to him. She was the one explaining it to me, and sounded pretty on board with the concept.

I asked her how she talked to Josh about the idea of going on trips with him, to try to understand if that was the issue causing this misunderstanding—and it was hard to tell. I'm never in their conversations about that, and I've never talked to Josh, only Debbie. She says that Josh and Jonah never really had any kind of friendship and that this might be part of the issue. It might be that it's a limit set so that they don't feel obliged to fund five vacations a year, even though that's never been the situation and isn't the actual case here. She understands Josh's frustration here, but doesn't want to change a rule for what she thinks will be an edge case.

Small spaces and doing polyamory harder

One of the biggest preconceptions about polyamory is that we must be in deep competition with our partner(s)'s partners at all times. While we discuss metamour relationships in greater depth elsewhere, let's take a moment to discuss the logistically most challenging time and space to embrace relationships with metamours, residing in small spaces.

Especially in cities, but in any location where apartments are common, folks may end up cohabiting in smaller spaces. In my study, only 16% of multipartner households lived in apartments or similarly small spaces, but that's consistent with the American population rate of doing so, which is 17%. The rate for my study may be slightly higher, because I gave the option of living in two or more units of a duplex or apartment building and had several respondents who were large polycules of many adults and some children living in two or more units connected or very close together. Those folks combined with regular apartments are a total of 23% of respondents.

The thing about polyamorous cohabitation in smaller spaces—even without being three or more people, but as two people who are polyamorous—is that generally it requires a level of kitchen table practice of polyamory (where partners, metamours, and telemours are comfortable in each other's company) and contentiousness that can be avoided or apologized away in larger homes. Where we have explained guest rooms and additional bathrooms and plenty of space in Chapter 3, partner selection and willingness to share space are king in small spaces.

Perhaps folks have a fold-out couch and there are agreements about who it is that gets the fold-out or futon—whether it's the visitor or the person who hasn't brought the visitor. And there may be agreements about scheduling and whether dates only happen at the same time such that there are a minimum of nights on the fold-out or a minimum of hearing kissing or other activities (and agreements about those activities when partners are home—many people are super relaxed about kissing but not at all relaxed about hearing sex through a wall, for example) in order to better manage time. These kinds of agreements can be hard to maintain in the long term but are necessary to maintain for some folks—which is part of why partner selection is such a big deal. Folks who really understand that sometimes there are schedule changes and these changes are no one's fault are essential to making polyamory work in small spaces.

So too are people who are willing to at least be friendly in passing with their metamours and come up with systems and signals of how they want to interact. All the apartment dwellers I spoke to mentioned their metas and their relationships with them in the follow-up interviews before I brought them up. The ability to have some kind of cordial interaction, even if it was to have an intentional "ships-in-the-night-" style connection, was important. One woman, Mary, explained to me that she worked opposite shifts to most of her non-nesting metamours and made a point of leaving snacks and notes to let them know they were welcome in her home when she wasn't off work, even if her work and sleep schedule meant that she mostly didn't meet people until they became long-term relationships for her partners.

People in these apartments mentioned their metamours in negative contexts sometimes too—the metamour who couldn't or wouldn't comprehend that the walls are incredibly thin in their apartment and was constantly *just* waiting until folks fell asleep to come home with their partner in the stumpiest heels anyone had ever worn and having very loud sex; or the metamour who treated only opposite-sex relationships as real in their mixed-gender polycule. Sometimes, apartments are in dense enough locations that they have the advantage of escape in case of conflict. If you're in a "real city" and a safe neighborhood, you can go to the coffee shop or for a walk and get out when the person who doesn't get it or is on your last nerve is there, in a way that you can't in a suburb. But that isn't true everywhere; sometimes your apartment is just small and you're just as car-bound as you would be in a suburban house—you can just hear more neighbors.

If you must get yourself and your partners into a kitchen table situation then you remove the possibility of parallel polyamory for your partners' comfort. In parallel polyamory, relationships are held relatively separate, and metamours avoid interacting with one another. In my blog, Ready for Polyamory, I define parallel polyamory slightly more broadly, as relationships in which a polycule does not have an intentional focus on entwining their relationships; and individual pairs of metamours get to decide whether or not they have relationships at all, much less close ones. Conversely, kitchen table polyamory is when there is a distinct focus on entwining the relationships and metamours spend lots of time together and have their own friendships. Living together in a multipartner household is its own micro-kitchen table but in small spaces, the entire polycule is forced into a broader kitchen table situation, because there's nowhere to go without an enormous outlay of money for hotels unless folks get on the kitchen table page.

Being on the kitchen table page means being on a page of careful communication, of willingness to consider the problems that come up, and being considerate. Boundaries have become the trending watchword of relationship communication—but boundaries we establish with strangers and people who are treating us badly are boundaries we enforce and reinforce differently than boundaries we set with those we love and who are generally treating us well. What do I mean by this?

I mean, boundaries are all things we set for ourselves, about ourselves, to set and protect an emotionally and physically ergonomic environment for ourselves. But if we're telling someone who loves us about a problem or a conflict—if someone we love is raising their voice too much in conflict and it's triggering me and making it hard for me to communicate my issues with them, for example (an actual boundary of mine)—we can tell them gently, and give them chances to learn about it and improve, instead of cutting off contact if they get it wrong. Whereas if a stranger or a person who has been behaving abusively continues to harm me by not listening to a boundary I set about not continuing to yell at me, I can say I won't be yelled at, leave the conversation, and not talk with them anymore. But I won't stop talking to a partner (or never talk to them again) about the same thing. I might take five minutes to regulate, and tell them so. That will likely remind them of this boundary, and they will probably not violate it for several months afterward and only overstep if they are triggered or dysregulated themself. In a case like that, I can find it forgivable. It's different than doing it on purpose or repeatedly or to scare me.

As a different example, if someone says they need space, we can ask what they mean, and that response and their clarification can be described as a negotiation of their boundary—but this negotiation is meant with love and good intention so that we don't violate the spirit of the boundary. Do they mean they don't want us to speak to them about the issue at hand? About anything? Is it okay to send them TikToks? For 20 minutes? For a day? Until they say so?

Again, these are conversations and ideas we don't necessarily have to have with anyone, and definitely not with someone actively harming us or strangers, but with a close friend or partner who is engaging with us in good faith? It's a good idea to help set boundaries more clearly and to communicate more fully by engaging thoughtfully. Boundary discourse has become individualist and while boundaries are personal—you do set them for yourself, and they do protect and define yourself—they act in relation with other people and you need to be able to express them to others. The importance of expressing them to others is that healthy relationships exist in the Venn diagram of people's boundaries—and healthy kitchen table relationships, polyamory in committee, exist in the Venn diagram overlap of still more people's boundaries, which is more likely smaller.

In general, nested polyamory in small spaces is doing it in hard mode—you've added a layer of complexity and requirement because you remove a layer of choice from yourself and your partners. You have to hope your partner selection makes that Venn diagram more like a stack of pancakes and less like a traditional Venn diagram.

CHAPTER FIVE

Making It Your Own

The Polyamorous Home

Personalizing your home can be one of the things we most take for granted, but also one of tasks we least consider when moving in with someone. When worrying about how cohabiting with someone will work, choices like who will sleep where and how many bedrooms there will be are a clear place to begin. But a "landlord special" whitewashed apartment with nothing in it doesn't feel like anyone's home yet—and it's the job of the folks who move in to give it character with their belongings and choices. (Although, sometimes, not too many changes, according to terms of the lease.) When you're polyamorous and moving in together, sometimes you move in to the new place together and get to make your choices at once about how to add character to your space, but sometimes, as with monogamous couples, one or more of you live in a place and the rest of you are joining. What can folks do in these cases to make sure that it doesn't just feel that a partner has rented the guest room, but rather that the house is now everyone's home?

One of the things that matters for this is how people *use* space. Are you a family that gathers and spends time in traditionally public rooms? Does everyone gather in kitchens, around the table for homework and dinner and cooking, and with a bustle and hum of different activities for much of the day? Or is your polycule's "kitchen table" actually the living room? Are you always around a game table, or sipping coffee or cocoa on the couch watching shows or on your phones together? Do you set up several surfaces around a living room so folks can be doing different things in the same space, but it's that camaraderie of folks sharing the public rooms?

Or, like Daniel from San Francisco and his polycule, do you default to living in your bedroom? If given a choice of how to spend your time, do you retreat into private and self-defined spaces, and leave "public" spaces for mealtimes, with most activities being easy to shift into your room? He described to me their apartment search, and how he and his two partners had actually chosen to flip the arrangement of rooms once they found one they were looking for, and make the largest room (intended as a living room) into the bedroom shared by two of three partners. One bedroom is used as a bedroom, a dining room is their living room, and a second bedroom is a home office. More important than the actual layout of their apartment is the way they as a family use their space. All the partners are folks who functionally "live in their rooms," with an open-door habit, and who spend a lot of time together and mostly use the kitchen and official living area only for eating in. Daniel assured me this was habit not policy: "These aren't rules or about being in each other's business all the time, but we're open and hang out together in each other's rooms or our own, depending what we're doing—there are bookshelves and a seating nook in the big bedroom, and some art stuff in my partner Charles's room, for example."

That might be shocking or incompatible for folks who live similarly to the way I do these days. I use my bedroom for sleep, sex, and maybe an hour of relaxation in the morning or evening before and after sleep. In smaller apartments or in differently shared living arrangements, I have been more of a "learn to live in my room" person, but it always feels like a retreat to turn "off" a sense of being with people—something that generally one hopes to reduce in planning use-cases in your own home. As somebody who doesn't worry that much about my room, and wants the "rooms we live in" to be nicer, I've often opted for bedrooms that just hold my bed and dresser, and not worried about whether I'm sharing them, or sharing bathrooms. When I lived with my ex-husband in a one-bedroom, I was quick to say, "Oh, whoever is having a date can use the bedroom, I'll sleep on the couch if someone's over and I come home." And I meant it—a scenario that is maybe not typical for folks. But having an apartment we could afford with a very nice, spacious living room and kitchen to host friends for coffee in the afternoon or make a dinner for each other or a date in, in a good location, was more important to me than a second bedroom.

Hopefully, before moving in together, you have some idea of whether you use space in similar ways; or if you don't, whether they're at least compatible ways. Assuming that you have, and if you're folks who "live" in public rooms, making sure people moving in get some chance to put their own spin and mark on these rooms (if they have the resources to) is important. Things like not banishing all of a partner's items to their room (a metamour of mine has a collection of skulls made of various kinds of rock and crystal that are on shelves in their living room that come to mind; or a survey participant mentioned making equal space for a partner's sports memorabilia and a collection of figurines she's been given since childhood); sharing bookshelves or adding more so that everyone's books are represented; and making space for a desk or table if someone does work or crafts from home so they have a place to leave their half-completed projects in a contained way; all can include someone in a space. In a kitchen, "space being yours" is likely in the details, and may only matter to someone who cooks, or someone who feels like life happens in kitchens.

NICOLE, MATT, AND JOHN

Nicole, Matt, and John are a triad who have been together for three years. They've just moved in together, and the process of uniting their two apartments' worth of stuff into one home was one of both combining and editing. Nicole told me that she found it "maybe silly but also pretty essential" to include small appliances from both apartments when they moved in to a house. As the hinge, she'd previously been the most "at home" in the two apartments, even if she only technically lived with Matt before. Integrating aspects of John's kitchen, by using his red kettle and matching toaster, and getting new rugs for the kitchen that brought together the red and grey of the different small appliances from the two places, made her feel like she'd connected the two houses, and "made it easier for both guys to feel like I didn't just throw out all of anyone's kitchen." Both of them cook more than she does—"I'm the head dishwasher," she explained to me, "so while I helped with organizing and setting up, I'm definitely not the person in charge in our kitchen day to day." I asked Nicole about where their family spends most of their time, and the living room was their answer—they have a large combination dining and living room where they play board games, eat, and watch TV on their own, with John's non-nesting partner, and with other guests.

So far, we've focused on public rooms, because of the (very privileged and polyamorous) assumption that there's some chance that someone might have their own bedroom and a certain amount of autonomy in setting up that room. But as we addressed in Chapter 4 when we talked about small spaces and the way practicing polyamory in small spaces can be rewarding but also "hard mode," lots of people don't have their own rooms, or even two bedrooms for every three adults. When we're sharing bedrooms as well, the use of rooms again matters. If you want to "live in" your bedroom, but it's a small room and there are three adults sharing it, this gets harder—you may have to change your habits about where you spend time, spread out stuff into more rooms (and accept the going to get them part of changing your habits), or decide that this space/home really serves the family you've built. This is a case where being compatible but not necessarily the same in how you use space can be handy—a person like me who just sleeps in a room moving into a house where a room-liver has used up most of the decorative space in our shared bedroom is fine, I'd just need living room space for my bookshelves and yarn.

Most of my follow-up interviewees talked to me by email or over the phone, but a few took me on video call walk-throughs in their homes, and the little details people chose to share as they did so were remarkably varied. Some folks wanted to share clever things they were doing with bathrooms to accommodate partners or kids. For example, one family had built-in cabinets along where old radiators used to be, that they'd set up as cubbies for non-nesting partners who use the bathroom with regularity at the far end and for the folks who live there at the end nearer the sink. Another showed me their house where kids had the "master bedroom" and adults had two bedrooms around a jack and jill bathroom. Yet another person told me the backstory of purchasing furniture for their living room with their partners upon moving in, because they all came from roommate situations and it turned out that they owned a washer, dryer, two beds, a kitchen's worth of things and a full dining set, but only a TV, nothing else for the living room.

The rocking chair from someone's grandmother's house, in the same room as their metamour's pride-and-joy recliner and a couch the polycule bought together made an eclectic but remarkably cohesive looking living space decorated in warm tones in Lynn's Texas home. She walked me through their home's details (craft room and home office combo, plus two bedrooms shared between three adults, for the ability of flexible schedules and one of them to bring non-nesting partners in, and art they'd gotten each other as housewarming and anniversary gifts).

These little differences, which are so hard to give anyone concrete advice on how to implement because they are essentially personal, are the most-cited key to making folks feel like they live in their new homes, and not like intruders or guests. If you can, take some time to think about what makes you feel at home, and how you use your space, before you move in with your partners. Make some deliberate choices to inject each member of your polyamorous family into the spaces they use most, and, where possible, make little purchases (budget is less often cited as important than visibility and daily use) of items that are mutually decided on so things are "ours" not just "yours" or "mine" in a home that partners will now share.

CHAPTER SIX

That's So Meta

Metamours and Scheduling

Managing metamour expectations

Metamours sharing space once they move in together should be no big deal, right? We've talked about the roommate principle and treating your partners like roommates first, and it should be easier to do that with metas who you aren't dating. But people can underestimate the way moving in together can change metamour dynamics, and the way a nesting dynamic can shift other relationships in a polycule.

People have a very natural proclivity to forgive partners quickly, to give extra grace to people they love. Unless folks who are moving in together have a very relationship anarchist notion of how their network is constructed, people raised in Western cultures tend to prioritize romantic partnerships in a way that discounts friendships. Metamours, even cohabiting ones, tend to be placed in the bucket of "friends," a lower-hierarchy bucket than partners. So household problems can get mentally shifted onto our metas' shoulders; partners can get forgiven more quickly than metas for issues in which they had equal responsibility; and our cultural narratives about friends and roommates (or worse! the ones about romantic competition) can creep in around our interactions with metamours. Even if everyone who lives together is involved, if they date outside the house, nesting changes the amount of time they might potentially spend overlapping with their metas.

There are lots of descriptive theories of how polycules are shaped or work and living together is the most kitchen table activity that could be defined, pretty much. People who live in the house might or might not resonate with the term popularized by the Multiamory Podcast for the closest kitchen table polycules: lap-sitting polyamory. If the extended polycule (additional partners who aren't in the nesting unit) also prefer a kitchen table style of interaction, a nested household often becomes a center for that. If only one arm of the polycule prefers that and other portions prefer a more parallel style of relationship, it can become a matter of conflict in the household. When one person's intention was "I wanted to live with my partner, and living with my meta was a comfortable part of that," and the rest of their relationships are parallel to that nesting partnership, but it turns out their partner and meta are very kitchen table and so there are lots of people around the house often, it can become stressful.

The obvious solution, of course, is to communicate and figure out what middle ground everyone can live with. But usually it feels to each person involved like their meta is controlling their lifestyle a little too much (even if the hinge is involved in the decision-making). The person who prefers kitchen table (and to host) feels like they're being asked to change plans and to inconvenience others on their end of the polycule, and the person who prefers parallel feels like they're having to beg for private time in their own home in a sufficient amount.

It's a balancing act that hopefully people would cover when they talk about how they like to live at home and how and how often they prefer to host or not. These are questions that individuals need to balance between themselves, preferably before they move in or as they make agreements upon moving in. Having a discussion about how often guests can come over, only to find out that one person in this conversation excludes non-nesting partners from the category of "guests," can be a rude awakening for someone who doesn't intend to spend much time with their metamours or telemours, for example. But, also, someone who doesn't consider those folks guests can't then turn around and say it's rude to guests for one of their nesting partners to go seek out private space when those people are around—that's just taking time for themself. It becomes a matter of conflict resolution. Which priorities matter most to whom and how much? These are very individual issues. I can't give you a perfect formula for every household. I can give you some questions to ask yourselves in a conversation before moving in.

- How much private time do you need in a week? In a month?

- Do you like hosting at the house? For small groups? For large ones?

- Who are your "could drop in anytime" people? Which social rules apply and don't apply to them?

- If folks are over the house, how do you feel if not everyone who lives there is part of the event? Is your answer different if you've got smaller or larger groups over?

- The kinds of issues addressed more in depth in Chapter 3 about partners staying over can be covered in this conversation too—how much private space do you want if you bring a partner you don't nest with over, do you want folks to vacate the house for an evening? Is retreating to their room sufficient if you have separate rooms? Do you want to all have coffee together in the morning?

- Are your feelings about hosting similar or different for polycule members, friends, and family?

For some people, all three of these last are similar; but for many, family is more stressful or polycule or individual members of extended polycules may come with additional baggage because of cultural messaging around how we "should" feel around "sharing" our partners. Being "polyamorous enough" that we want to live with some partners doesn't mean we've miraculously unpacked all our cultural/social narratives and shame around all partners or everyone they're seeing (or every phase of those relationships)—so our answers to those questions above might vary. Just giving consideration for each other's levels of introversion and extroversion and coming to agreements and compromises around things like not considering it antisocial to take decompression time while another household member has a partner or a small group of guests over can be really sustaining for a network of relationships.

This can be a pain point where giving our partners grace can be easier than giving our metas the same benefit of the doubt. Whether it's metamours who don't nest with us who we place the blame for disruptions on, when we need to resolve them with a nesting partner; or a metamour with whom we also nest who has a different preference than we do for how we manage guests and schedules, misplacing blame on a meta can be easier than we'd like.

A good self-check-in to run is: Is this really a meta problem, a shared problem, or a partner problem? If it's a shared problem or a partner problem, make sure to address it with the partner as well so you aren't building unnecessary resentments against your metamour.

Beyond actually putting an event in the calendar, or discussing in the abstract whether you have an expectation that people be available for a specific event, deciding what is "an event" that needs discussion versus what can "just happen" around you is a step people often skip, but which can avoid a lot of strife in households. People assume that everyone is coming from the same background and norms, when a lot of the time even people raised in the same area or by folks of apparently similar backgrounds have very different expectations around how to spend time at home. The questions posed above about what kinds of time you want to spend with whom in your space are a great starting point, but for many folks aren't a natural way to begin these conversations. (This is one of the upsides for me as a neurodivergent person who is always looking to make expectations transparent—polyamory requires more of these conversations than monogamy tends to, and neurodivergent people tend to require more of these conversations, so the two go hand-in-glove to some extent.)

Calendars

Beyond time with guests, plain old managing the schedule of the household is a common pain point for folks. One of the biggest things that change when non-monogamous people become nesting partners for the first time is scheduling—especially if it's in a dynamic where not all members of the household are romantically or sexually involved with one another. Polyamorous people do scheduling gymnastics—the polysaturated among us, if also working jobs with variable schedules and carting kids to activities, could be called the Simone Biles of Google Calendar. Ideally, everyone has been doing their own individual scheduling gymnastics, with visibility to one another through something like free/busy access to their calendar (or, if everyone is open to it, just a shared calendar) prior to move-in.

Often, when people move in together, they expect scheduling magic to take place. There is a certain (mononormative) cultural narrative in which moving in together is the natural "next step" after already spending most of your time together anyway. Non-monogamous people may or may not be following this relationship escalator as written when moving in together. As we discussed in Chapter 2, for some polyamorous folks, moving in with multiple partners is a way to proceed up that escalator in multiple relationships; for others, it's a sideways step off the escalator and logistical choice. For everyone, but especially the former group, cultural narratives about owning your partner's passive time once you live in the same space creep in. "If they don't have specific plans I've heard about they'll be spending that time with me" rapidly turns into an assumption of "We have all this time, we don't have to make specific plans" and then disappointment when, in fact, someone else has made specific plans and you did not.

When an already nested couple opened up, they either learned this lesson the hard way, and now schedule their time specifically—leaving the newer nesting partner to fall victim to the pattern on their own time—or they dated together to avoid this and now presume that moving their (polyamorous) sweetie in will work the same way their monogamous relationship did, just +1. If it turns out that their sweetheart still has plans with outside partners, and that those aren't always on a strict calendar day, or that they didn't book a date with their newer nesting partner for over a week and now they miss them, it can be a hard lesson to learn. This is especially likely if you're not explicitly calendar-sharing. Some households (about 20% of the follow-up interviews I did in my survey) have weekly meetings to talk about when folks will be home or out so they can plan meals or split chores if they don't have a standard division of that labor. Others don't have formal sit-downs but share digital calendars and discuss plans in passing with partners and metas.

Generally, folks either have individual calendars that they share visibility for with all household members, or they have a "family calendar" where everyone dumps all their events that affect household members.

> As an example, my coparents and I, although we no longer share a home, share a calendar for our children—it has all of their activities, school spirit days, summer camp weeks, when I'm taking them to the beach for a week in the summer, when my coparents are taking them to Disney for four days next fall, and so on. It also contains any deviations from their standard schedule—days I'm working late and need my coparents to get them from school and I'll pick them up, or vice-versa. When we all lived together, it also included nights any of us were going to be out of the house, whether with each other or alone.

If one dyad has been living together previous to the household expanding, and only one member of that dyad has been in charge of both people's calendars—or their whole family's calendar—that's a yellow flag. While it's fine (in fact, good) to want a household shared calendar or to prefer to have a shared calendar you can all view, one dyad operating as a unit for scheduling when others don't tends to indicate there will be problems of passing the buck by the partner who doesn't manage their own schedule, or problems of unexamined couple's privilege in this dyad. Either of these leads to inequity in the household and the larger polycule in conflict management. As we discussed in earlier portions of this book, while most "polyamorous problems" are in fact couple's problems having ripple effects outside a particular dyad, the shared home is one of the few locations where this is not necessarily true, and schedule management is one of the subjects where it is most often an individual's problems having ripple effects to all their partners.

It can also be a place where metamour relationships that are generally good can become fraught. If Alice has been managing her and Bob's calendar, as well as all the activities for their kids, and Alice and Bob haven't fully separated the labor of their calendars before integrating Carol into their household, it might make Carol feel like her options are to maintain a separate calendar, or also be "managed" by Alice. Alice manages both their social and work calendars and keeps track of family birthdays that are coming up. Since they opened up and started going on dates alone, they both have the ability to edit the calendar, and Bob does a lot more actual work around the house—all the outdoors maintenance, and a good chunk of indoors chores—and they feel that's equitable; but Bob generally only uses the calendar if he meets someone new he wants to date, and hasn't in several months. Let's look at both these possible scenarios where Carol, Bob's partner of almost two years, is going to be moving in.

If Carol wants to share visibility on calendars but keep her own, this might help with not feeling micromanaged, or as if Alice views her as an additional household responsibility to manage. Since she has a partner who isn't moving in (Dave), the separation will let her copy to her calendar events she's also going to so that Dave knows she's busy, without having to share all of Alice and Bob's schedule with Dave. The downside is, it might make Carol feel less enfranchised as a household member to not fully share in a household calendar that contains the children's events, especially if she is taking on a coparenting role. It maintains a strict division of "Alice and Bob" the unit, and "Carol" the individual, rather than creating "Alice, Bob, and Carol" the household.

If they all want to share a calendar, empowering everyone to actually use it, make changes, and input events becomes important. If Carol is sharing in parenting duties and picks up the kids and they come home with a flyer from school about a spirit day, she should add it to the joint calendar, not leave it on the table for Alice. The same is true for Bob. They have to work together to break the norms of a "one-mom" family where one person is doing the logistical legwork. The parent doing these logistics is not always mom, but most frequently is, and in most heterosexual couples that open up and have this issue it is the woman maintaining the calendar and doing the series of tasks known as "kin-keeping" for the couple.

Polyamorous households increase the amount of "kin" to "keep" but also the number of hands to do it—if you're willing to break norms. Letting a digital shared calendar do some of the leg-work allows all the adults to participate and then review together what ended up in the calendar in a simpler way than having to make phone calls to every adult in the household whenever there's an invitation to do something. If folks don't actually take each other up on the opportunity to help with this work, odds are that resentment on the part of the person taking on the mental load of the household schedule will build up; and potentially from the outside on the part of non-nesting partners—imagine how frustrating it would be to have someone you're in a relationship with tell you "I think so, maybe... I have to run it by Alice" every time you tried to make a plan with them. The responsibility sits with the partner in the middle to use the calendar they're handed to actually use it in that case, and with Alice to forgive slight slip-ups the first couple times people "use the calendar wrong" in favor of encouraging its actual use.

I've very briefly alluded to kids' events and coparenting,

and we'll talk about how those complicate schedules more in Chapters 8 and 9, but if folks aren't coparenting, it can also be helpful to have a "kid calendar" or "kid event color" in the shared calendar so folks know which events apply to whom. Using different colors in a shared calendar for the different people involved can be helpful for events that involve a single person being out of the house, but it gets unwieldy quickly and it's often more useful to throw an event description in that includes who is attending.

Once you have systems in place for scheduling and have determined folks' boundaries around what time in the house should generally look like, you get to combine that with the physical and space considerations we talked about in Chapters 3 and 5 to come to a mutual understanding of how and when common spaces are going to be used, and what spaces are private. Life is unpredictable, so there will always be the special occasion for which everyone reshuffles their calendar, or an emergency for a polycule member that folks show up to be supportive of, or a middle-of-the-night kid stomach bug that takes all adults on deck to handle (especially if you've all got it too), but covering how things work most of the time, or in current conditions, or in your preferred version of current conditions, as you settle into a new nesting partnership can help a lot.

What about jealousy?

As a subculture, polyamory loves to imply that one can outgrow, outrun, or avoid entirely the experience of jealousy. Frankly, this makes more people feel like they're doing poorly at polyamory (because they're having a bad day, felt a negative feeling, or don't have an ideal reaction to something) than it does to convince monogamous people that we're correct about anything. Everyone experiences some jealousy sometimes, but often not in the situations you'd assume; and the key to getting through it (because it's just a feeling) is to not give it the power of defining your personality. We can have feelings, be curious about our experience of them, and learn from them without then claiming we don't experience them or are enlightened beyond them.

People assume there will be jealousy if you're living with your partner and a meta because it will be certain that you'll witness more of their affection for one another than you would have otherwise. Most people I spoke to for this study knew and anticipated that, and had a pretty predictable level of struggle (or not) with jealousy and the partners they were actually nesting with (more on that in just a second.) But many had more struggles than they'd anticipated with jealousy and their partners' non-nesting relationships after they moved in together.

Why the non-nesting relationships? Well, partly because a lot of our cultural messaging about marriage and living together is about how boring it gets and how tired our relationships are and how downhill things go, so regardless of how good things are in reality, it's a lot more anxiety-inducing to see your partner choosing to spend time elsewhere and having new and exciting experiences. And partly because a lot of us have a certain amount of protectiveness of our house and our space—and having other people in our space can be activating to begin with, so we're more primed to notice a twinge of negative feeling. And last, because it's easier to blame the entity of the relationship or the person of our non-nested meta than our partner whom we love when our partner and meta do something inconsiderate.

There are lots of ways this can manifest. The jealousy researcher Dr. Joli Hamilton distinguishes envy and jealousy in her research, with envy being about "objects, possessions, luck" that someone has that we don't have—a fundamentally two-sided thing, where jealousy is interpersonal and about fear that includes a third person (Hamilton 2019). This means that feeling a twinge of envy that a meta has more money than we do is a different experience than feeling jealous (and underlyingly fearful that our partner might leave us) because this meta with more money seems to pay for lots of really nice dates we can't afford. This is one of those subtle differences that matters when we're trying to process a feeling or have a conversation with our shared partner about what we need—it's reassurance about our relationship, not for them to stop seeing people who happen to make more money than we do.

For a concrete example, let's consider a family from my survey who have very small kids. As we'll get into in the chapters on parenting, toddlers and babies are, in some ways, simpler because they typically do go to sleep; and if you're comfortable having partners at the house, you can have after-bedtime dates with greater ease for kids who live on an earlier schedule. But if your kids are at all high need or you default to one person needing to have these kinds of dates while everyone else in the home gets opportunities to go out "because the kids do better with you at bedtime" or the parents haven't let each parent build their own routine for kids to get used to, it can cause resentment among the adults. Sean from my survey included in his email some concerns about this as his family's biggest struggle with cohabiting:

> We've done a good job living together but had to figure out a new schedule entirely last year. It started because one of my partners, who was the biological mom of our kids, was first breastfeeding and then pumping milk for the kids. They got used to her as how they fell asleep and everyone else was OK for middle of the night wakeup but not bedtime—so we'd give her and her other partner the house at least one night a week but not have her go out. That became habit and we didn't realize how long it had been and that it was bothering her until it became a big problem. You

don't know what you don't know until it's a problem, especially with kids.

When you're on the outside this can sound like an obvious solution—make sure to give all partners some time off. But deep inside, kids having phases and stages that you're handling that are not always easy and can change as soon as you get a system in place (particularly for babies and toddlers), buckling in and handling it can feel like the only option. Every family will have their own system for managing time and scheduling, but there are some possibilities that might make it a little simpler for folks. Some people make set weekly schedules with time out of the house (or in the house, with other partners or grandparents taking kids out of the house) such that everyone gets a set amount of time that is neither kid time nor work time. Others analyze on a longer timescale, which can be more useful for handling the uncertainty of very small children (who may need all hands on deck for a sleep regression one week) or folks with shift work schedules (who may not have dates that line up with their non-nesting partners in a predictable way week to week, but can find three in a month). For folks who want the longer analysis, if you find that there's unevenness over time (as in Sean's family), you can choose to track time away to make sure all adults take it evenly. Jessica and Joe Daylover have a worksheet they created for their polycule's use for this, which they made available through their platform Remodeled Love and then in a more refined form in their book *Polyamory and Parenthood,* where they track what they call "autonomous time"—alone time that isn't for paid work. The idea is that if you realize halfway through your tracking period (however long you've set it to, they default to a month) that someone is way behind another parent in taking their autonomous time, you can work it into the schedule coming up to get some balance back.

With three or more adults this is sometimes easier and sometimes harder! If one partner is really consistent about scheduling their time out with a non-nesting partner (or has one where others don't) it can be easy to blame that non-nesting partner for "dragging them away from responsibilities" on a hard night, so reconnection and balance become important. Not basing all our alone time and time away on dating and making sure we give each other time out of the home (or at least time away from home responsibilities, whether they're kids or dishes) can really make a big difference in how we feel about our partners' relationships.

Protectiveness of homes and spaces manifests in lots of ways, but the most common one is folks who are concerned about the way their bedroom gets used. We've talked about alternative space solutions for this in Chapter 3, but how do the discussions and emotional management of this happen? First, the discussions need to happen between the people who reside in the space. If you don't agree with your partner or partners who have concerns about how a room or a bed is used, speak up right away. Don't wait until you're in a relationship where you're champing at the bit to change a rule you've agreed to. Talk to them about what it is that they're hoping to achieve by having no one but them sleep in a shared bed, or no one have sex in a shared bed. Most of the time, there's an alternative that can meet much of the underlying need, like making sure bedding gets changed (including a mattress pad for folks who get grossed out about fluids, for example), removing blankets or having dedicated blankets for sleeping, having one's own pillow and a separate one for guests. When it's about wanting to believe in a sense of privacy in the house, talking out the ways that your partner has privacy, that no one is violating their things or going through things but that this bedroom you share with them is a shared space and you want to collaborate on how to use it is often effective—but not always.

We talked earlier in the book about when folks have different ideas of who is a guest or what counts as visits, and this can be very connected to that. People feel differently connected to one another's partners, and so letting go enough to let those people into our bedrooms—rather than into the public parts of the house, where we are used to letting guests exist—can be a big vulnerability.

Marcus told me that in their household, he thinks that issues with having non-nesting partners come over for overnights or sexual dates became fraught because they are a vee, and the hinge whose partners both live in the home is the one who had concerns about people in shared beds:

> It came to a head and eventually we changed our rules to just involve a lot of laundry and clean sheets and mattress pads, but it took my metamour having a partner where they had nowhere else to go for dates, so hotels would have been really expensive.

Practicality, and then the experience of the thing that the hinge feared not being that bad after all, with a mitigation step taken, ended up winning out in their home.

> But there were a few weeks—maybe a little more than a month—where it caused a lot of problems because they had no place to go back to, no one was shelling out for hotels, and we're not teenagers hooking up in cars, so it was a real drag for the relationship. Pointing out to her that this was effectively controlling, even if she didn't mean it to be, and that it would be on nights when she and I were on dates so it's not like she's home alone or listening at the wall for them, plus the first couple times going very smoothly and

> her going to nice fresh sheets in the room she shares with him the next day, made it all work out.

If they'd agreed ahead of time, they might have skipped the weeks of disagreement, trying to find money for hotels, and seeing if they could channel their inner teens for car make-outs. But sometimes experience is our teacher, and it can feel like a really minor thing to say yes to, if everyone we're seeing currently has a place to go back to, or our partner is upset and negotiating a solution that respects their boundary feels difficult in the moment.

Most often, during the study, I heard about jealousy in a very abstract way, or from partners who dealt with its effects in their household but weren't the jealous ones. This makes sense—I was having casual interview conversations about people's homes, not in-depth relationships with these people. In my work coaching polyamorous folks over the last several years, and the 17 years I've been polyamorous and in community with other polyamorous people, I've seen jealousy in a much more intimate and personal way, which is why I've so confidently asserted that it's common but not the core issue for most people. Jealousy is a check engine light—it can mean that there are problems minor or major, and it takes our effort to consider and determine which it is, and what's underlying.

Dr. Hamilton's determination that all jealousy involves interpersonal relations and some kind of fear is true—but what's driving the fear? Do we fear because of a problem or unmet need within the relationship at hand? Because of an inequity between our relationship and the other one of which we are jealous? Because of an insecurity in ourselves? These are the most common causes, and inequity and insecurity are the core of the two examples we've just discussed. If there's an unmet need in your relationship(s) working with your partners (or, in a household, your partners and metamours as applies), to meet those needs first will be necessary to calm jealous feelings.

What if it really doesn't work?

If for any reason—jealousy, just truly not vibing, having incompatible personalities, what have you—you and a metamour really decide you can't be in the same space, this is still alright. There's no requirement that everyone must be best friends with their metamours. Many of us, in the course of our polyamorous journeys, will have a metamour with whom we just don't vibe—with whom things sit just a little off for us—and we prefer to keep a little distance rather than maintaining a kitchen table polycule with them. If we've been used to close, kitchen table or lap-sitting connections with our metamours, it can be disappointing or jarring to realize that we can't make all our network's relationships fit this mold, and the first instance or two of needing to figure out and navigate setting appropriate parallel boundaries—even garden party relationships (in the space between parallel and kitchen table, preferring to see metamours only for occasions) or relatively close parallel ones—can be challenging.

The first thing to take into consideration is the idea of sharing your expectations and boundaries openly and before you let feeling like you don't want to be buddies (but maybe this meta does) boil into resentment. Part of what makes these conversations potentially tricky is that setting boundaries around interactions can feel like a personal rejection. Especially for those of us who struggle with conflict or tend to people-please, the instinct to say "Oh it doesn't matter" and go with the flow until a higher level of interaction proves repeatedly uncomfortable and truly unsustainable is a strong one.

I'd like to advise you that it's easier to set an expectation of less time together (or fewer one-on-one meetings, or otherwise a lower interaction relationship with a metamour) and walk it up very slowly over time and have to pull back just a little when it's too much, than to go along with all of a hinge's or meta's suggested activities regardless of our apprehensions and come to a place of resentment about them. If you've hit the point of "I've been trying a very long time and I can't stand it anymore," you will probably need to have a conversation about a more extreme, siloed version of parallel relationships (which will likely have more of the conflict, defensiveness, and pushback you didn't want) than if you just acknowledge, when you first feel it, that you need some space. Being able to share your desire for a more parallel relationship in a way that doesn't say "I find you intolerable" and that isn't rude is often a worry. Remember that you don't need to give a detailed backstory and explanation to express your preference, even (or perhaps especially) if you're making a change to how things are going. A sample script of how you might bring this up with a meta could be:

> Everyone doesn't get along perfectly with some people, and I think you're a good person. [Hinge] and you seem very happy and well matched, and I wouldn't want to get in the way of that at all, but I'd be more comfortable if we took a little more space from one another than we have been. What that would look like for me is [strategies and suggestions you've come up with, like not hanging out alone, not just the three of you hangouts, timing dates at similar times to your activities, examples below] but still being open to [whole polycule activities together, seeing each other in passing as part of dates with hinge, etc.]. This is important to me and I hope you understand.

With phrasing like this, you're softening the "taking it personal" of the conversation while leaving space for discussion of which of the things you're open to they also are amenable to, acknowledging that a relationship hasn't gone perfectly without placing blame, and reassuring about your respect for their relationship with your shared partner.

The next thing (which many of us might do first) is to consider your and the meta's relative entanglement with the hinge and, based on that, what some reasonable mitigation strategies and boundaries are. If the hinge has some particular expectation of polycule entanglement, you'll need to discuss your feelings with them—and because they care about you, even if it takes them a minute to come around, they'll recognize that respecting everyone's boundaries is necessary to keep the relationships running smoothly and help you determine how to approach any shared activities. If you recall, boundaries are about the things that are within your control—your actions and reactions—so recognizing how the lay of the emotional land may affect those is important. (For example, a boundary is not "Don't talk to me that way"—that's a request; but it could be "I don't remain in conversations with people who talk to me that way"—your action that you'll leave a conversation if the condition takes place is enforcing your boundary.)

In all cases, if you'd been trying to be more closely connected, like by text messages or by trying to go out for the occasional coffee or drink, removing yourself from group chats and asking the meta to please only contact you by text in case of an emergency is a reasonable way to step back to a parallel place—and having a conversation about what big group events still feel okay is worth doing. Do you, for example, think of a monthly Dungeons & Dragons group as a small group not a large one? If you're the one who wants the space, you should be the one who leaves the group, in most circumstances.

Remember, like we said above, boundaries are about our own actions and not about banning people from things. While there are some situations (like when you cohabit with the hinge) where rules may come into play to help enforce boundaries, generally setting a bunch of hard and fast rules with no room for fluctuation will backfire over time. Talking about specific activities where you're likely to overlap can be a prudent step, but so can dealing with things as they come up, depending on how high or low the frequency of such events is. If you don't share a huge amount of social overlap, or it's all because of the hinge, it's often pretty safe to ask the hinge to be mindful of schedules and not over-planning beyond that.

If you nest with the hinge, the challenge is in setting and enforcing your boundaries while being mindful that you aren't setting your partner and meta up for an implied veto via logistics and rules—take into account whether your shared home is the primary place they can date for one reason or another and whether there are workarounds and mitigations for those concerns. Some examples of changes you might suggest to the hinge and your meta include:

- Not communicating with your metamour about the logistics of their being present on a given day a lot; leaving it up to the hinge to plan their dates. Sometimes, nesting partners (especially female-socialized long-term nesting partners) have a history of being their partners' "social secretaries" along with their other roles in their lives, and polyamory can be part of how they realize that's what's been going on and then back off from that role. Not running your partner's calendar and setting a boundary with a meta that each of you should talk to a partner directly to plan is a fairly common transition-from-monogamy boundary that people have to set.

- Scheduling dates when they'll be at the shared home

and you have plans out of it; if you have another partner whom you see outside the house regularly, or a hobby you do every couple of weeks or once a month, that could be an opportunity for them to have "night in" as opposed to "night out" alone time.

- If the shared home is big enough (or sounds don't particularly bug you, or throwing on headphones is all you need, because you just don't want to hang out with this meta, not don't want to think about them), just do your own thing and ask not to be invited to participate in (for example) a shared dinner or a board game or a movie, they have their date and you have time to yourself elsewhere in the house. This works best if there are multiple bedrooms so you aren't being turned out of your own space, or you have it to retreat to if partner and meta are using the living room for a movie, for example.

- If you have boundaries you want to shift around whether or not sex will be okay with you in the shared home and it was something that was previously established, try to co-create rules around it rather than just handing them down, and try to be reasonable about how they would be enforced—you don't have to agree to anything you aren't comfortable with, but keep in mind that if you make an agreement like sex being okay in the shared home if it's when you're out, and you come home hours earlier than expected, it's not the hinge's fault for not mind-reading your early return.

- Be polite when you do cross paths with the meta in the shared space; being parallel with someone but "in their domain" can feel odd, and tiny neutral-to-positive interactions can keep everything feeling less like a personal judgment and more like (which it usually is) just not having the emotional bandwidth to make a ton of new emotional connections. (If it helps, think of yourselves as roommates or guests at the same hotel meeting over the buffet breakfast—"Good morning, the weather's nice today, isn't it?" and a smile is a lot nicer than scowl, glower, frown, and a shove past.)

- If you've passed the point of "really can't handle even seeing them," maybe because of trying to do more contact than you're comfortable with and not expressing it until too late, or being pushed to do more than you wanted, consider setting a trial period for doing so in large or public settings and going from there. These settings are often the most neutral ground available to you, and trialing it for six months can give you a sense of whether and how your emotional state is shifting.

If the metamour nests with the hinge while you do not, most of your choices around suggesting things be more parallel are around shared social time and choosing whether or not you enter the hinge's space:

- As above, but in reverse, you can ask to only schedule "nights in" in the hinge's home when the meta has a night out planned, whether with friends or partners, and offer your own home or nights out as an alternative date activity at other times.

- Figuring out if you're comfortable being in the same space but not interacting with someone can be very trial-and-error—I have had parallel relationships where those ships-in-the-night relationships were comfortable and ones where they were very awkward, and there is no pattern in them that I can discern to advise you with. Be ready and willing to adjust how much time you spend in the hinge's home if it's shared with a partner who you're generally parallel with, because sometimes the "wave hello and disappear" move feels natural, and sometimes it feels like a jump scare is about to happen, and if it's the latter that's not super sustainable.

- If you're long-distance with the hinge and you want to remain parallel with the nesting partner, this is harder; as it requires either that the hinge only visits you or that the nesting partner be turned out of their house for a period of time. Offering to help mitigate travel costs that are higher for the hinge now can be a solution to the higher burden of travel now on them becausc of this change.

- Being polite and civil to metamours is the only thing we owe each other as people in thc world. No further relationship is required. If you want to date the hinge in a way that never walks into their home and carefully negotiate public events so that you minimally interact with their nesting partner, go for it. If you think their nesting partner is just fine, but you just don't want to be expected to be their friend independently or go out for drinks or whatever, also, cool, just negotiate it. Most people are relatively reasonable about these things, especially if it's said outright.

If you and this meta are comfortable enough that large groups and occasional social functions are possible but the smaller ones we just talked about are not comfortable, consider negotiating ahead of time whether either or neither of you will attend them as the hinge's date and what kinds of expectations you two have around them. Will deciding who goes home with the hinge ahead of an event ease tension? Does the hinge have a suggestion for how to handle large events where no one is "the date" that is more comfortable for them, like all arriving and leaving separately? Are holidays included in your vision of that, or something that you'll decide closer to the time on an as-needed basis? It's okay to not know ahead of time, but these are the questions that will pop up over the first year or so of being in a parallel polycule.

The transition to a new way of interacting with someone in your relationship network can be challenging, especially if it feels one-sided or like the hinge wants a closer relationship between partners and it's a struggle to set boundaries, but it doesn't have to be complicated. Figure out what logistics make sense for your situation, and if you're comfortable with your meta alone, in small groups, in big groups, or not at all, and have a conversation accordingly. You're all adults and it will work out, maybe with some adjustment as everyone finds their metaphorical footing.

CHAPTER SEVEN

All About Money

This book is not in any way intended to be financial advice for the folks who pick it up, but many polyamorous forums online and discussion groups in person have featured some variety of the question "Well, but what do you all do about money? We don't all make the same amount." So this chapter is going to reflect the variety of strategies my survey respondents and coaching clients have shared with me and consented to being anonymously used.

Before we engage too deeply with any of the strategies for dividing or combining finances, I want to make a note of how monogamous norms around finances are also shifting in our culture. It used to be that it was an absolute certainty that if you married, you would share a bank account, share credit, and otherwise combine all financial matters. Women couldn't open a bank account or hold credit without their husband as a cosigner in the US until 1974, so this was not just habit but requirement and certainty for many years. While change has been rapid culturally, and both married and unmarried women now have some independent finances, many people still see combining finances as a rite of passage when marrying. The shift in this norm is happening. Fully separate bank accounts are held by 23% of married Americans, and 34% have a mix of joint and separate accounts, with the percentage increasing in younger demographic cohorts. The studies on this do not consider relationship style as a possible reason for couples wishing to maintain some financial separation, but do consider several pragmatic reasons couples might, including:

- disagreements about how to save or spend
- widely differing incomes
- being generally low-income (68% of individuals making $50k or less a year keep some money in joint accounts, 83% of those making $100k or more do)
- those with a mix of account styles generally say that joint expenses should come from joint accounts and individual expenses shouldn't.

All these reasons apply just as much to polyamorous families as to monogamous couples—the math sometimes gets a little more complicated when you have three, four, or five adults rather than two, however.

Some people jointly, some separately

Let's talk about the most common scenario that folks reported in the survey: some people in the household have fully joint finances, and some fully separate, with 39.2% of my respondents to the initial survey indicating that this was the case in their household. In follow-up questions, it was always the case that one or more married couples had combined all their finances and did not want to separate any of those from one another, and an additional partner, or additional married couple, did not want to either join them in a further, more joint, household account. In some cases, this meant there were two bank accounts being used in a household: one for a couple, and one for an individual, to cover a household with three adults; in other cases, that there were three or four bank accounts but that at least one of them had two adults with fully merged finances using it.

These systems tend to have in common that folks talk a lot about money. Keeping some of the finances separate should mean that each person is paying many of their own bills (car payments, gas, insurance, dates with partners outside the house, for example), but it requires a lot of planning for the shared bills. Is there a schedule for who's picking up the groceries? If one person's schedule means they do the shopping for the whole family, do they have to ask folks to pay them back in turn? How are people adjusting for income? Is everyone paying each other back for the electric bill? Do you have a spreadsheet?

DAVE, ALICE, CYNTHIA, AND MARK

I spoke with Dave, a member of a quad (four-person relationship) from California, who shared the experience his large family of four adults and five children had with financial matters. It was a quad that formed out of two married couples, so they entered with two sets of joint finances and didn't want to further create additional joint bank accounts to manage the household. One couple was on the mortgage; they assigned many of the bills into the name of the other couple and then did the math about how much the difference was between those expenses before deciding who would pay for groceries, for example, in a given month. This meant that most months, Dave and his wife Alice were paying for utilities and a greater proportion of groceries, and his partners Cynthia and Mark were covering the mortgage and a lesser proportion of the groceries.

They all managed kid expenses together, as they coparented and homeschooled their children. (Cynthia and Alice met in a homeschooling mom group, and moving in together had allowed them to have one more adult go back to work more hours, as only one parent did fuller-time teaching of the elementary-age kids and the older child went into public schools.) The adults managed their car payments and student loans within the couples they were in, as well as any pre-existing debt they had.

The methods for sending money back and forth between couples were less of a problem for these folks because they tracked all the bits of expenses that needed to be covered and talked about them as they happened—if something got out of balance or someone was short on cash, they simply sent a bank transfer or a Venmo or grabbed some cash. The key, as Dave expressed to me, was not getting too bent out of shape about individual purchases:

> If any one person decided alone that something was important but they couldn't afford it, that's when conflict happens. But if you can say "Oh, I've got it covered," there's no argument to be had, or if it's something we all agree is necessary, like replacing something broken, that's easy. The problems are when someone wants something new or extra that not everyone agrees is needed and they can't afford it.

This theme comes up in lots of families I spoke to, no matter what system for sharing expenses they used—if something isn't necessarily shared but you need financial help with it, it becomes a possible source of strife. "All of us being used to sharing in a smaller unit, and still worrying among ourselves about if we're willing to take on debt or not, helped ease some of those worries."

All people separately, but some expenses joint

This scenario is what happens when folks want to have a big, upfront conversation about what constitutes a "joint expense" and then talk less about money. It involves more planning at the front end, and often includes a joint bank account that all household members pay some portion of money into. In my survey, 26.6% of respondents indicated that they followed this model. It tends to be popular because it can be implemented in either flat-rate or income-adjusted ways, and it leaves a portion of folks' money to their own discretion rather than in joint accounts. Several of the people I spoke to in interviews indicated that either they or their partners had reservations around feeling like someone was observing their purchases and financial decisions, or like they had to justify everyday expenses, and that keeping some finances separate helped with this.

Items that typically ended up joint in these scenarios included: rent or mortgage payments, utility costs (electric, water, internet, gas, etc.); shared media accounts; groceries; if everyone coparents, costs for children (preschool, sports, clothing, medical costs); major household item purchases (furniture, paint); household maintenance costs (higher for owners than renters); and often a family cell phone plan. Families had a wide variety of other items and concerns they included in individual agreements—vacation funds, college savings, retirement plans, down payment nest eggs for a next home, needs specific to your family—but the unifying theme was that all these folks sat down and agreed with the people they were building a household with and decided these were the costs they were tackling together rather than independently.

Items that most often wound up independent for partners or metamours included: cars and their fees and maintenance (notably, households in areas where cars were less essential or one was shared among a whole household and other adults used public transit would move cars to shared categories); schooling and student loans of adults in the household; costs of children who are not coparented within the household; dates; clothing for adults; minor household purchases and incidentals. Obviously these are not exhaustive lists, but they give you an idea of how the conversations begin.

Folks figure out together what they want to pay for together, and how much money that will cost them monthly. They talk transparently about what they make and decide if it feels fair to divide it by a flat rate (say, four adults each paying 25% of the total), or if a little more math has to be done. If everyone's income is within a certain amount of one another, or everyone makes significantly above the local comfortable cost of living, it is simpler to do an even split, and folks will default that way. Many people I spoke to choose to do this, even if sometimes it is then less convenient for one member of the household or requires other adjustments between themselves (like having other partners always pay for within-the-household dates so that a household member who makes less still has a comparable level of disposable income left).

Still others choose to take the household expenses number and everyone's income and do a little math to divide it proportionally. Let's say that all your joint expenses total out to $6670 a month, that one of you makes $120,000 a year, another makes about $80,000 and two make about $60,000. (You can get as granular as you want—we have calculators for this—but for the "example in a book" purposes here, I'm going to try to stick with pretty round numbers.) This means you have a total household income of $320k, and each person's income is 37.5%, 25%, 18.75%, and 18.75% of that income, respectively. So you're going to pay that percentage of those expenses. The person with the higher income will pay $2501.25 monthly, the second highest $1667.50, and the two with the lowest will each pay $1250.63. The extra couple cents there come out in the wash. At this income level, folks may feel like those few hundred extra dollars aren't a big deal and they want to all pay that 25% rate, but it may be really important. Sometimes, one or another person has very high student loans they need to pay off and they don't want to make that a household budget line item by folding it into the combined finances or by straining their ability to pay in taking on those few hundred extra dollars a month. Other times, it simply means that everyone in the household still has discretionary money left over after both household and personal need-to-pay expenses are met. We're talking about pretty high income levels in this example to make the math easy to understand, but this system was most often used in my survey by folks who were cutting expenses tighter to their budgets and wanted to make sure they were doing so as fairly as possible.

One of the families I interviewed, a triad from Seattle, shared with me that this was how their finances worked, and that sorting out what costs should be joint was actually the biggest challenge of their first year living together.

BEDLESS IN SEATTLE

Jane, her partner Liza, and Liza's partner Britney moved into a two-bedroom apartment in Seattle in 2019. While splitting utilities, groceries, and rent was obvious to them, there were some costs that weren't so obvious. Liza had a car that both her partners borrowed sometimes to visit partners who weren't in the area—should they split maintenance and payment costs or just throw her gas money? Because Liza was always sharing a room with one partner or another when she was home, if she wanted to see non-nesting partners she either had to stay at their place or get a hotel room—would the triad split these costs as a function of their living situation or would this be a cost Liza picked up? The women decided that gas money would be sufficient but that if hotels became a recurring cost for an ongoing partner they'd work together to either figure out schedules so it didn't have to be, or to pay for this cost together, because it was not their intention to stick one member of the household with a big expense just because they didn't want a bigger home. Their lack of guest room and how to split the costs associated got figured out, but took some problem-solving.

They also had to internally address questions of what kind of furniture, decorations, and appliances were "shared" and not, over the first several months. Whether aesthetic upgrades counted as upgrades that needed to be shared was occasionally a point of contention. Britney made more than Jane and often wanted to get the "nicer version" of things, where Jane and Liza were content to continue using a version that worked that they had from previous living situations and only get new, or a version to everyone's taste, things that no one had brought. After some uncomfortable conversations, "we were able to get to the heart of it—that Jane felt like it wasn't 'our' house until we decorated together, but that I wasn't okay spending so much, and the balance I wanted—of her paying more for things if it was more her priority—felt emotionally bad and like a rejection to her. We figured it out with time, but it took a lot of monthly check-ins before we got there."

Keeping all finances separate

Some people don't want a joint account for anything—the fees associated with keeping an additional account open without a direct deposit don't feel worth it, they don't think they're really sharing that much, or they think it all comes out in the wash anyway. This approach was taken by 20.8% of folks who responded to my survey. In follow-ups, I spoke to relatively few people who implemented this. However, from emailed responses, it seems like most folks who implemented this do so a lot like people who are used to having roommates—they say "Remember, it's rent time next week" and everyone Venmos the person who's actually paying their share (or an equivalent for other bills). One or two indicated doing some more complicated math around some people having some bills in their names and others in other people's names, but most often it seems that this method is implemented when a home is owned by one person or one couple and one or more partners move into it and are paying into the bills, particularly when (if a couple was involved initially) that couple already kept their finances separate.

Households with children who were not being coparented by all adults present were more likely to do this than households where either all adults were coparenting or where there were no children at all, but my sample was not big enough to draw statistically significant conclusions on the correlation of how finances and parenting style intersect.

All finances completely joint

Just over 13% of my respondents indicated that all of their finances were completely joint. In conducting follow-up interviews, this seems to be most common in the case of relatively well-off households who are doing significant forward financial planning. They combine resources and plan for retirements together, and, in the case of some folks, look at how best to protect assets in inheritance together, and more. Because three or more people are not a standard formulation for accounts in most cases, or for property ownership (several of my respondents indicated that they needed help figuring out ways to set up mortgages or transfer ownership of property such that it would be owned by all partners), there's a significant investment in setting yourself up for success.

This often includes people who create LLCs (Limited Liability Corporations) that hold their property—this does not work in every jurisdiction but it's a functional way to give multiple people control over a property without requiring multiple signers on a mortgage in a way that lenders are loath to allow. Making all partners or all household members partners in an LLC with ownership or signatory power is a way to work around the fact that it is challenging to get a mortgage for more than two people. The reason I note that this is mostly a concern for well-off people is not that only well-off folks buy houses (although in 2024 in the US, that's an arguable point), but that doing loopholes like hiring someone to help you incorporate appropriately and help your company purchase property legally rather than simply having an individual or a couple from within the household purchase and everyone else pay them back (or sign a lease agreement for a room within the house) is a tactic employed by folks with privilege of both money and information. In the UK, the decrease in housing affordability is just as striking—London flats per square meter are topped only by Hong Kong in price, and much of the country is not far behind. So polyamorous folks everywhere I spoke to are absolutely factoring housing costs into their financial decisions with their polycules.

All finances joint, by replies in some cases, meant some finances, as in the group above, with a bit of misunderstanding of what "all" meant, because folks had independent retirement accounts, independent savings accounts, independent car payments and credit cards. But for others it truly did mean that everyone had added everyone else in the house as authorized users on each other's cards, had signed on each other's car loans, and had visibility of, if not access to, each other's savings. Whether the distinction between "some" and "all" finances joint is meaningful is really individual. People have their own concerns about money and their own backgrounds that drive financial needs and financial conflicts. What folks generally aren't prepared for when they move in together as a polycule is that there is more to money and money matters than just managing your household budget month to month.

What about "non-essential" spending?

Special interests and hobbies

As in both case examples noted above, it's not the day-to-day spending or immediate bills that became points of contention, but items that folks had disagreements about and differing perspectives on. While some of these might feel "too minor" to some of you to bring up in a book like this, I think it's important to mention them because so many folks I spoke with brought up at least one variation—a hobby or recurring bill or cost that only one household member had that they considered a non-negotiable bill, that everyone should have an equivalent of and everyone *could* pool resources for, but not everyone in the household *did*. The most common one folks mentioned was gym memberships and personal trainers—if one or two household members were avid gym goers who were happy to get "a family plan" and make sure it was accessible to all members of the household, but not all folks in the household wanted to use it, it could become a point of contention. Similarly, expensive hobbies that had the possibility to include travel or frequent participation in events that only a couple members of the household participated in and that included expenses had similar effects (whether those expenses were for the actual events or for childcare around the events, so that non-participating household members didn't become resentful of time taken away). The exact hobbies varied, but the effects did not.

This especially became a point of contention when two unmarried household members participated in hobbies/travel/competitions and others did not, because they were then more likely to regard them as household expenses. Married household members more often had separate-from-other-household-member finances to handle costs of their interests, if they had a shared interest other partners didn't; and folks who shared an interest with partners outside the household were more likely to regard this as a cost that they should individually cover (maybe with the help of their external partner) rather than treating it as a household expense. People who have previously been solo polyamorous for some prolonged length of time also appear to have less of a habit of making the costs of matters that are not household bills into shared costs.

This appears to be less of a problem for people of broadly lower socio-economic status (or at least from a background of lower socio-economic status) than for those who come from more money. A great deal of "being good with money" in the middle-income and upper-middle-income area that many respondents reported being from seems to be reflected in nickel-and-diming friends and loved ones in how one splits a bill ("owing" $8.50 after a sandwich out that one covers, for example) rather than generally deciding if one can afford an experience and participating or not. People of lower socio-economic status tend to set themselves up in homes they can afford, with bills and outings they can afford (and use credit and not tell their friends and lovers that they're doing so when they can't), and take turns covering things, rather than take bills to pieces percentage wise, except maybe in an initial breakdown of who can afford what in a conversation about the full household cost. They're more willing to have the initial conversation about how money will work in the home, to not have to have a hundred small conversations about "owing" one another—where folks from richer backgrounds think of owing one another as a default state and that money moving is a natural side effect of having money. Of course you owe your friend $25 from brunch and you're picking up the next dinner with Bob and Susan and you know who is behind whom in terms of the bills. Our culture begets awareness of money, but in very peculiar ways that are particular to different classes, and class conflict within a polycule or household can be a big source of financial conflict.

Vacations and external partners

Not every household is a closed polycule, and how to fund dates out with external partners can be a serious point of contention in many polyamorous households. What folks spend with partners, whether partners outside the home pay or things get split, and what dates look like can be a stressor that doesn't occur to people until they live together. Many people who open up out of couples have dealt with this to some degree before they meet someone who they're interested in moving in with, but if one has primarily lived alone, or lived with roommates rather than partners for a long time before moving into a polyam household, it can be an adjustment point to have to consider how external partners impact the bottom line. If this household is the kitchen table portion of an otherwise garden party or parallel polycule and you only see external metamours at big parties and events, your primary concern about them might be how much your partner spends in going on dates, outings, and vacations with them. While trying to balance things 1:1 is not recommended, making sure you meet the needs of others in your household as well is a good way to reduce conflict around "but *they* get *all the nice things* and I have *all the drudgery*."

For households who include their own internal vacations in household budgets and thereby make the household budget bigger, leaving discretionary funds smaller for household members, it can create some tension around whether that changes the priority or hierarchy of non-nesting partners. If you can't afford to take non-nesting partners for a weekend away this year, but went on a beautiful extended vacation with your nesting partners, is that a budget concern, is it a priority and next year you may prioritize differently, or is it a hierarchy issue, and every year you'll vacation with your nesting partners first and *if* you have funds left over you'll consider going somewhere with your secondary or non-nesting partners? This is an issue that can cause tension and conflict within the household and within the larger polycule, depending how direct you've been with external partners. As those relationships get more intense and longer-lasting, folks tend to have more expectation of landmarks like vacations, like participating in life events that might require travel, such as weddings or school reunions. Then deciding which you'll participate in, which you won't, and whether you're leaving yourself appropriate discretionary funds in a "some finances separate" system, or how to handle tension over only one or only some household members having these expenses in an "all finances combined" system becomes important.

But note that, much like those hobbies or gym memberships, if everything is coming from one pot but only one person is benefiting, it can be something everyone is on board about because it all comes out in the wash eventually—you'll all have an expensive hobby or a weekend away, whether it's a weekend with the girls or a weekend with a girlfriend someday—but it can also be a point of resentment or annoyance in the short term, because some day is a matter of years at times.

Different members of households also have wildly different ways of approaching these issues. Some people try to reduce their spending to the minimum if their household partner doesn't currently have an equivalent expense in mind—if, for example that person doesn't have a $200 gym membership plus classes. Or they may say with their own partner outside the household, "I won't get the nicer four-day weekend away, I'll get the simpler two-night version and make sure we drive home promptly." Others, relying on the fact that the tide will always turn, and that their partner will be happy for them, lean in to their opportunities and do them up if they can afford them. Still others figure out how to divide them such that they're paying more for outings at times when their partners or household members also have positive opportunities and their outside-the-home partners are taking on more of the bill when that isn't the case. As with so many other things in polyamory, it is a choose your own adventure story.

Special occasions

Whether or not special occasions and holidays involve financial conflict seems to correlate to two issues: whether folks moved in together relatively quickly, without observing each other's styles of how to mark holidays; and how much money is available at the holidays. The second is not something I can give you any real tips on. Capitalism sucks. I make a lot of holiday and birthday gifts for the people I care about and it still costs too much, along with costing a lot of my time. However, the best indicator of not having financial conflict at holidays seems to be having similar gift-giving priorities and not conflicting over who should be given things and of approximately what value those gifts should be.

This saves no one from many other holiday and special occasion conflicts—like whose house you go to when, and whether you instead host everything yourselves and invite scores of older family members who may not attend because you're upending tradition by doing so—but it does save you from a bunch of money worries. (The hosting may, incidentally, cause other money worries, especially if you spend a lot cooking for a bunch of extended family members who are "maybes" that turn into "nos" at the last minute, but that's more often emotional conflict or a need for emotional support and reassurance.) Financial concerns for things like "Will we throw a commitment ceremony for the other relationship(s) in our household?" varied a lot among respondents to my survey, and folks largely found ways to do these cheaply or waited until they could afford a wedding-adjacent event to throw one. (Several mentioned avoiding the word wedding with vendors to save money—if you'd like a tip.) In general, non-gift holidays, and big special occasions that required spending were better received by households than, say, someone deciding this was the year to go all out on everyone's gifts—even if they were using their own bonus to do it.

On the negative side of special occasions, several people mentioned medical bills as a source of financial stress for their household—and as a chronically ill polyamorist, I relate. It can be either helpful or terrible that medical bills come individually. You have to then navigate if these are household expenses or personal expenses. For many households, these are clear household expenses—much as groceries or a water bill are, they're necessary care. But when only one person or one insurance-dictated family is costing thousands of dollars a year...it can be a point of stress, to say the least. For many people, living in a household together eases this stress, because you can divide the cost among more people; but for some who have never had to consider the real costs of being chronically ill—or even if not ill, just the costs of different types of care, for example if one person has dental work that needs doing—it can be a financial shock and that can lead to resentment and conflict. This is unfortunately a growing issue in even outside the US, as medical-system reforms lead to less coverage or more privatization of specialists.

What do you mean, you don't ask about money?

In sorting out financial style, just as with monogamous couples, polyamorous people can run into conflict because they communicate about it differently. As with so many relationship issues, this can be complicated by the fact that there are a greater number of moving parts because there are more people involved. The addition of nesting partners to a household that had already established patterns of how finances, bills, etc. were handled can also upset habits and patterns. Folks who decide to upend their existing patterns by, for example, signing a new lease even if they live in the same place in order to include new partners can be doing their best to build entirely new patterns that include everyone.

Sometimes, however, the new patterns still include or are built around conflicts. If, as we were discussing previously, household members have very different preferences about how they talk about money, it can create anxiety for one or more members who have different styles. Nowadays, when it is easy to check bank accounts constantly, folks with anxiety around finances can keep a close eye on joint accounts, and this can either help assuage anxiety—or cause conflict. A Boston-area polycule I spoke to was in the process of disentangling their finances because too much visibility was causing greater conflict and anxiety than it was resolving:

> One of my partners has a lot of anxiety around money—which always strikes me as funny because we're better-off than I've ever been, but worse off than he's been, so I guess it makes sense—and so we ended up combining pretty much all of the household finances into one account in 2021. The rest of us in the house thought this would be great, because he could see what we were spending and we could skip the step where he checked in about

> little purchases and wanted to know how everyone's finances were and was double-checking that we'd have enough for bills. He'd be able to see we did. But none of us were ever going to develop his habit of sort of asking the house in general if it was okay to make purchases of irrelevant size—not appliances, not vacations, but like "a niece or nephew needs a $20 birthday gift" or "I'm grabbing lunch at the diner with a partner." And so he kept texting or calling us all to check if every tiny purchase was real and what it was, and we all can't stand it. It caused tons of fights, as he's insisting he's doing what's best for us and we're wrong for not asking about every little thing. So we're all taking our money back apart and creating a bills account we deposit into and letting him make the payments out of it for utilities and rent. We hope it's going to help, along with continuing therapy, sometimes together.

For some people, having those recurring little conversations about money is exhausting and too much—death by a thousand cuts—and for others, like the partner in this story, it's the balm for anxiety around money. When that partner lived with only one other person, it was simple to just let him manage money for the dyad and give him a heads-up if purchases were getting made today—but in a big polycule house of five where he had two partners and two metamours? It felt stifling to people to have him try to exercise similar levels of control over money. The conversations about that feeling of control often became heated, and he felt a certain degree of entitlement to the control both because it was rooted in his anxiety and because he was good with money and concerned about keeping the household within their means—where some members of the polycule were having trouble coming out of debt. These concerns are legitimate on all sides, and listening to one another and coming to decisions that work for your home will be very individualized, but generally speaking, as in most relational areas, taking away autonomy from others in the name of assuaging anxiety will not go exceptionally well.

The bottom line

There are as many ways to organize spending and saving as there are households and there is no magic about polyamorous people that makes this less the case. Do you plan to combine all of your money for the rest of time? Do you wish to keep it completely separate and give each other money for bills? Which things in between matter most to you?

If you have substantial assets, you should absolutely be seeking out professional assistance in how you organize them, and get a will and decide if putting money in trust makes more sense for estate-planning purposes. If you don't, you should still think about what costs you're happy to take on and which you aren't, and how your household plans to save in the medium and longer term. We're going to talk more explicitly about how costs for children get covered, or don't, in parenting chapters coming up.

I hope the variety of ways folks divide and combine their finances have given you some things to think about. All of these considerations are in the category of "things to think about, as you make plans to merge households."

CHAPTER EIGHT

"But What About the Children?"

Polyamorous Parenting

We've mentioned kids in passing several times throughout the previous chapters of this book. Parents may have been champing at the bit—ready with the natural next issue or next solution that comes to mind when you add children to the mix—and non-parents may already be irritated with me for winking at and then sliding away from the Child Issue. (If the latter is you, you may skip the next two chapters. They are about parenting and its attendant concerns. Your child-free world will be intruded upon much further here.) To all of you who have been waiting patiently for the "parenting" part of this book, thanks, we're here for a couple chapters. Every polyamorous parent gets asked "But what about the children?" an exhausting amount of the time, and we're here to talk about some of the practicalities about how you may "what about?" your particular children and partners.

Who will be parenting?

There are so many choices to be made about who in a home (or a polycule) will be parenting children, and depending on the age of your children, the question is one you can consider from many dimensions. (If the children are still hypotheticals, it's a conversation you should have even before trying to conceive if you're doing so deliberately—and a "what if" conversation you probably should have briefly had along with your birth control use if you aren't, but that you'll need to revisit if the pregnancy is unplanned, as nearly half are. We'll cover pregnancies later—let's return to already present children.)

Many folks approach polyamory from the position of having already had children before they opened a pre-existing relationship—or at the time they wish to have children, have only one partner they wish to parent with, and all other members of their relationship network are on board with this. The "kid question"—or, more correctly, the parenting question—becomes more complicated if folks want to change their entanglement level with some partners. Is there a level of everyday involvement or entwinement at which you are no longer comfortable with someone not being a parent to your children? What, for you, is the distinction between parent and caring-involved adult? Do both (or all, if you're already coparenting) of your child's current parents agree on these issues?

If the children's current parents agree on the possibility of there being additional parents, and that there is some threshold at which involvement creates de facto parents, you all have to keep each other apprised of the progress of relationships that might become parenting relationships. If the essential difference is one of amount of time someone spends with your children, and someone is creeping up to that threshold, have the conversation before it's a fight "that your girlfriend is being an extra mom two nights a week without doing the really hard parts of this." If that sounds like a pre-cohabitation fight, it's because these often are. The Big Parenting Conversations are usually the hardest run-ups to a move in. They're incredibly personal, and we return to them later in this chapter.

Else-Marie and Her Seven Little Daddies

When we became parents, my coparents and I went looking for resources for normalizing our family structure for our child. If we were doing this today, there are plenty of newer resources I could now recommend to a similarly situated family, but at the time we leaned heavily on a few picture books about queer families and one out-of-print book we were recommended by Reddit and bought second-hand: *Else-Marie and Her Seven Little Daddies*. In this story, a little girl named Else-Marie has to overcome her embarrassment that her fathers (who for reasons that remain unexplained are much smaller than the other adults or children in the book, and all do things in a unit together, despite being tiny businessmen who have an undisclosed office job) come to pick her up at school. She worries about the teacher not understanding that they are little and that there are many of them, but nothing goes wrong: they stay for story time and pick her up uneventfully; everyone goes home on the city bus with no problem; and she, all seven little daddies, and normal-sized mom have a beautiful evening at home. Was it a perfect analog for our family? No. But did it offer a world wherein families that look different are still respected and acceptable even if they cause a little anxiety, much like the real world? Definitely.

I say "much like the real world" because, as we discussed briefly in Chapters 1, 2 and 4, although there are clear instances of stigma that apply to polyamorous folks and households, for the most part, people mind their own business and let folks make their choices, and yours will not be their problem. Like Else-Marie's daddies, you might be a bit of a curiosity, but you won't be worth comment from those outside your family most of the time. Within your family, chosen family, and emotionally intimate community are where the conversations and conflicts will happen.

The book doesn't address any of the questions the adults all asked each other about it that the kids never really bothered to ask us—like why Else-Marie's daddies are little, how her mama ended up with seven little daddies, what Mama's family thinks of her life, how the biology of Else-Marie and her family works, and more. That's because it doesn't matter to the kids, and in an ideal world shouldn't matter to the rest of us. They're a family, if they want to tell us their origin story it's a different book; Mama's family are opaque and we can assume they react like the rest of the world here. The equivalent questions are the first ones folks take into classes about polyamorous parenting or coaching sessions when they're starting to date polyamorous parents. "How will we come out to the world around us?" "What if we embarrass our kids?" "What if that embarrassment actually raises to the level of kids getting bullied?" All of these are real concerns—but unless your kids are already getting bullied for other things, their parents' dating is probably not going to cause it. You're going to embarrass them at certain ages just by existing; it's part of differentiation, and pretty healthy.

Moving in, and talking about it

The same advice that applies for moving in with kids when you're remarrying or blending families as monogamous folks applies for polyamorous folks:

- Create consistency in the kids' environment.
- Don't create big surprises and sudden shifts.
- Make sure the adults are on the same page regarding major topics like discipline, decision-making for kids, and prioritizing kinds of activities (and inform kids of changes to their rules or routines before they take effect!).

- And keep in mind that kids are KIDS, and that they are still learning the emotion-regulation skills that we as adults should be modeling for them (but might also be struggling with a little during a major transition like a move).

Let's look at these one by one. If kids only exist in a home from one partner or one family, creating consistency can come in several forms, but things like not uprooting their school district if you must move homes, not moving homes if you don't have to (just move a partner in!), keeping them in their after-school activities and having parents show that those are a priority over parents taking time to date, can go a really long way toward security and consistency. If it's a case where there are kids in two households that are merging, and you're all moving into a new space, or where some of them have to move, keeping them in some of their activities so they get to keep connections with friends and make gentler transitions can be really helpful. Making sure that kids get as much time to get used to partners and other kids being around (week-long vacations together, holidays together, partners being over for dinner and sleepovers frequently) can make transitions seem much less sudden.

Kids are extremely perceptive, and kids in our culture are acculturated to relationship norms! If you're trying to be closeted, they will be worried you may be getting divorced (and monogamous culture says time apart or "excessive time" with other people may mean that) and your coming out will be a relief at the same time it's a shock. Hopefully, if you're at the point of moving in with someone, you have come out to your children as polyamorous as a prior step to discussing someone moving into your home. The majority of folks I spoke to for the survey who had kids who moved in together had younger (age ten or under) children upon moving partners in. Those in the minority with older kids mostly got "Well, duh!" kinds of out-loud reactions from their children upon discussing move ins and relationship changes: "Oh, Dana decided paying for an apartment she doesn't sleep in isn't worth it?" one 16-year-old in Minnesota allegedly asked her mother. And while these somewhat sarcastic first reactions might underlie any kind of reaction to a move in, it's then up to parents and partners to continue those conversations (while giving kids space and respecting boundaries around processing). Parents need to make sure they get far enough into these conversations that kids have all the information they need. Kids need to know if a partner moving in is going to be allowed to make new rules for them. If that partner will be allowed full enforcement of existing rules. If anyone is going to expect them to change what name they use for this partner (and to what?).

All of those factors are things that you can (and ideally should) give your kids some lead time on. You don't need to give them adult-level visibility into your decision-making—they aren't necessarily parties to choosing whether a partner is going to be a parent, because that partner has first opt-out (although especially with older kids, giving them a voice on some issues, like what name they use for later-in-their-childhood-acquired parents, can be really powerful!). But make sure they know that this conversation is happening: "Hey, kids, we're planning on Dana moving in when her lease is up in three months. The adults are having a lot of big conversations about what exactly that's going to look like and we're going to keep you in the loop as more decisions get made, but we're sure that she's becoming part of our household, not just family in Mom and Dad's hearts." Doing this a couple weeks before you have concrete details to offer, and then a conversation with a lot of those details, can make older kids feel a lot more included. It minimizes the jump-scare-level surprises we don't want to give anyone but especially children.

In the name of minimizing surprises and allowing consistency, you don't want a massive shift from, say, kids never spending time with a partner to suddenly their being a full parent. If someone is moving from across the country, you want visits, video calls, and time together as a family to build excitement and familiarity as best you can. If they're moving from across town, that scenario where it feels like the partner barely lives at their own house is one way to slow-roll a move in and manage a transition. Whatever works for your family works, but the key is to make sure that the kids aren't shocked by the incoming partners and the role they may be taking on in their lives.

For the adults, these big conversations, some of which may be quite challenging, about "kid stuff" will be ongoing, but having some of them ahead of time really smooths the situation. Determining among yourselves the practical actions that distinguish a parent from a non-parent—and who will parent based on those definitions—is the first such conversation and also the one you come back to. What about, for example, someone who swears they don't want to parent but is happy to:

- clean up kid messes
- support kids with homework
- wipe butts of small children (or equivalent "gross" tasks)
- financially support kids by contributing to groceries, rent, and activities
- be present for kid milestones like graduations, birthdays, holidays

- help with medical issues kids have
- help enforce parental rules around kids' actions
- take kids to and from activities?

Where is the distinction? Is it that they didn't make the rules that they help enforce? That they don't (or didn't) pick the pediatrician the kid sees? If they do much of this, but not the finances, is that not parenting? If they do the list, but no discipline, is that not parenting to you? This is extremely individual, but also if you don't have a conversation about it and scope creep means that over time someone goes from "occasionally watches the kids alone, doesn't pay for kid things" to "parent adjacent and this conversation is much more relevant," it can be a much bigger source of resentment and conflict.

IVAN, CORA, AND JEAN

One of the families I spoke with was very concerned with decision-making powers and how many parents would become involved in their children's major life choices. Ivan, Cora, and Jean were a triad when they began building a family, and it was very natural to them that they were all equal parents with equal decision-making power regarding their two kids. When their triad broke up and all of them became seriously involved with other people, questions about the parental roles (or lack thereof) of those partners came up. Because they had three parents for their kids (including doing custody paperwork between the three of them for those kids—more about that in the chapter on breakups), adding additional legal parents was distinctly uninteresting to them. They decided that their new partners could take on caretaking roles to individual comfort levels, but would not take

> part in decision-making around financing activities for the kids, around medical choices and doctors for the kids, and around what schools the kids would be enrolled in; and they agreed that these newer partners would with time probably become consultants or unofficial parents, but the voting, decision-making power would remain with the three original parents.
>
> This has mostly worked for them. Their partners, who all live with parents (some of them in a multi-adult household, which is why I ended up speaking with this family) act as caring adults—they do school pickup, help with homework, remind the now tween kids to pick up their rooms, and more as adults of the household—but are called by their names, regarded as step-parents, and seen as a very slightly different category of adult by the kids. When the kids were four and five, Ivan's partner Leanne moved in with him and Cora, and the kids called her "my Leanne" as a term of affection since they already had a mommy and a mama. As they got older, they dropped the affectionate "my" and just called her by her name, but as small kids they showed their affection and her quasi-parent status by talking about how they were "going apple-picking with Daddy and my Leanne this weekend" and things like this.

If adults who intend to live together are intending to parent, and are getting on the same page about these decisions, determining how discipline will work is the biggest issue. While gentler parenting is definitely more the style currently than when today's parents were children, there's still significant variation in parenting styles on a spectrum from child-led/responsive through popular mixed gentle parenting and more traditional rules-based parenting to a stricter and more authoritarian style. This is true for monogamous folks, too, but among polyamorous households you can get a little more variation with newer parents coming into established households bringing their own ideas about it that changes how this reflects on kids—in follow-up interviews several respondents cited repeatedly making adjustments to this among the adults over the first year as the biggest struggle of moving in together. Knowing generally what style of discipline you intend to follow, whether certain parents (like the biological or longest-standing parents) have a final say if there's a conflict about what to do in a case that's never come up before or whether it'll be handled by whatever parent is there at the moment, or everyone will handle it collaboratively, are the kinds of things folks should try to talk about at the outset or be prepared to have as issues that come up.

What about emotional processing? These are all big changes, and big changes come with big emotions, most of the time. As adults, we tend to have coping skills for these—we know how to focus our energy on the positive, how to acknowledge that nervousness and excitement are related feelings in our bodies, that moving is hard but after we move we get to enjoy our new home—but kids have smaller frames of reference. We need to help them move through difficult experiences. It's our job as supportive adults (parents or not) to give them the lift they need to get through hard things. Just like we hold and soothe babies until they regulate, and we give toddlers names for emotions and help them realize what's happening so they can come out of a big emotional state, we can talk with older children about big experiences and that we're also having concerns and feelings and give them healthy outlets in movement, in safe adults to talk to, and helping them recognize signs that feelings are coming on so they can actually enact coping skills. (Teaching a ten-year-old to recognize that if their heart rate is up and they're hot, they might need to take a minute and count and figure out what's making them angry before starting to yell a few minutes later can save everyone a lot of fights a couple years later, according to psychologists.) If partners are moving in with us, or all of us together, these are large changes for our children that can come with a need to help them over some bumps.

Things that change with the age of children

I mentioned above about giving older kids more of a say in how move-ins happen. This is not to say that you're going to treat kids as partners in making these plans, but it does mean that as kids get older, they have more and more of a voice, and while kid concerns are often "felt" from the moment there's a baby onward, different ages and stages have different concerns and impacts on homes and on polycules.

Teenagers have opinions. They have their own space, they have their own things, they may be anxiously awaiting the moment they can leave or quietly hoping they don't have to (and that no one asks too directly so they don't have to admit such an uncool opinion). There were fewer polyamorous families with teens in my survey, and more empty nests that moved partners in as soon as they were sure kids weren't moving back in, but there were some; and the school-age-kid folks I spoke to will grow up into families with teens. The most commonly stated reason for having waited to move partners in was that teenage years are a huge time of upheaval anyway. As one woman, Jenna, in the follow-ups put it, adding partners as "...functionally step-parents they don't want, when they still have two parents? Felt like a lot, especially since this way we only came out to our friends and family, not also their friends parents and loose connections."

Teenagers are old enough to have an understanding they've formed out of the culture at large of how relationships *should* work, and if you haven't been active in counteracting that (if, like Jenna and her husband Rich for the first two years of their non-monogamous relationships, you were trying to keep the fact that you were polyamorous hidden from even your kids) that can make it a tough uphill climb to convince them that you're not just the weirdest and this isn't just impossible. Jenna's youngest is 20 now, and she's pretty sure that just keeping a guest room for when the kids want to come for holidays is OK, but not coming out to the kids until they were 14 and 16 and giving very slow-rolling information to them meant that by the time they moved their partners Amy and Larry in to their house, the kids had very firmly settled into an opinion that this was "the weird thing Mom and Dad do that we don't really talk about," and it becoming daily life has been a very hard switch.

When there are teens in the home, teenagers have an impact on space concerns the most of any kid age group. While many parents were happy to rapidly remove space from a teenager "when they moved away" (for college or into a first apartment), as with Jenna condensing her two kids into a guest room in the example above, unless folks were already living in space small enough that teens had been sharing a room their whole lives, no one in my survey was willing to make teenagers share rooms to make space for a partner or partners to move in.

Schedule-wise, teenagers can be high or low impact, depending on parents' support network and kids' independence and choices—a teen who learns to drive the minute they're allowed and then helps shuttle around younger siblings has a huge schedule relief impact for parents, as do kids who happen to have activities close to home and walk places. Kids who are less independent or have lots of activities that need adult involvement require more balancing of the schedule—the Google Calendar expertise I mentioned in earlier chapters becomes essential if there's more than one kid going in their own direction for sports, arts, academic activities, college tours, and social events with friends. Parents' social events often take a back seat after work, school, and kid extracurriculars. Nesting, and kitchen table polyamory can be popular ways to compensate for having less social time, but it's not perfect as a strategy because relationships need independent time as well as group time and often these strategies increase group time over all else.

Tweens and that "still a kid but not super young" cohort of school kids are the age that get the most benefit out of being in a polyamorous home. This age group, who tend to be extremely programmed with activities while learning a lot and going through big emotional and educational shifts, really benefit from what Dr. Sheff calls "polyaffective bonds" (see Chapter 4)—whether or not they have additional parents, having additional interested adults willing to chat with them about gymnastics or about the book they're reading, or to see the new drawing they've made, is really valuable to their ability and willingness to go deeper in these activities. At home, they tend to impact space concerns—this is the age where kids get bedrooms moved apart if they're going to. While in polyamorous homes that sometimes doesn't happen because space is at a premium (or public space is being prioritized or flex space like a guest and craft room or guest room/office), this situation often causes the adults to make decisions about whether kids are prioritized or adult comfort. As we briefly discussed in Chapters 3 and 5, it's up to the folks who live in a house to decide where they sleep and how to use their spaces, but often, some folks will prioritize kid space over either common space for everyone or a room being an adult space.

DAVE, EMMA, AND JASON

Dave, Emma, and Jason, and Dave and Emma's two children, aged 10 and 12, live in a "technically four-bedroom, but it's three and a basement" home in New Jersey. They had already needed to have a desk in the corner of their guest room for Jason to do some work from home when he needed to do paperwork; and originally they'd set up their home with the guest room, the kids in one bedroom, and the adults in another, and a basement rec room. When lockdowns happened in 2020 and suddenly all three adults were working from home, the basement went from den to school room/office for some of the adults. In due course, the kids went back to school, but only Emma went back to the office, and gradually both Dave and Jason moved office spaces down to the basement. While this is occasionally inconvenient (if they need to take a call at the same time, one of them has to go upstairs or shut the other out) it has mostly worked out. The opening up of the guest room space with no office in it if anyone wants to have a date over, with no chance that Jason needs to grab something out of there, has been really positive.

But now the kids want their own rooms, since they're getting older. Dave and Jason both bring dates to the house frequently and were a little unsure about how this would affect those relationships. Emma was very much in favor of giving the kids their own spaces and additional privacy, but she made very rare use of the guest room, having attempted to date outside their household a little and decided that she didn't have bandwidth for it. The adults had gone back and forth on the pros and cons and decided that since all their current partners had some alternate place for overnights to happen, so long as planning happened, they were willing to give up the guest bedroom so the kids could each have a bedroom, and just have a futon or pull-out couch in the basement for guests. At the same time, they pulled many of the kid items that were cluttering the basement office space back into those kid rooms, and gained "adult space" in the basement with that office, although there is "still a little discomfort around having gained public space and given up private space."

Kids in this age range typically impact schedules a lot, depending on the style of polyamory you practice and the availability of a support network for their parents. Taking kids to and from activities is by necessity an adult job—and depending on if every adult in the house is a parent, that changes the availability of parents a lot. Also, if parents have either family nearby or a broader polycule (whether the nested partners or non-nesting partners) who are available to help with things like babysitting to cover dates or weekends away or other private time, it's much simpler to make time for those things.

When they don't, it's tricky. One of my partners and I have dates that start at about 8:30pm on Mondays because that's when shuttling kids to and from activities is over—his nesting partners handle bedtime, but our kids go to different activities and adults work on different timing all week such that this is the night that works out for us. (Every once in a while, an aunt or grandparent is free to take a weekend and we steal a Saturday too.) Folks with less local family support often end up building it in their polycules.

SHANA AND JOE

Shana and Joe recently moved in with their partner Reggie. In addition to that, they live at the center of what he calls a complex intertwined network of relationships, with several children from each of their previous marriages. The kids are between 9 and 14 years old. Not all of their partners are deeply involved with the kids, but those who get the closest to them are, and do things like helping with school pickup, taking kids to and from activities, and watching the younger kids while parents are out on dates. All their family live three to six hours away, so while Grandma might be an option to cover mom and dad's (or dads') week-long vacation, she's not an option to cover date night if the whole triad wants to go out together—but a non-nesting partner might be. They run

> lots of kid-friendly local polyamory events and try to return the favor whenever they can—watching metas' and partners' kids so that those dates can happen in return.

At this age, chores and responsibilities are something kids are getting into more deeply, and even non-parent partners in the household may be impacted by helping kids become more responsible and part of the routines of cleaning, doing dishes, keeping their rooms nice, and so on. Are parents going to determine and set expectations with kids and then have any adult in the household being able to enforce them, based on (for example) a whiteboard chore chart? Are all the adults going to work together to adjust household expectations because kids chipping in is going to change what adults are doing, because parents were doing their own and kid laundry and now we're teaching kids to do it and expecting that of them? These parenting tasks are something that naturally shift as kids get older, but if you're adding parental figures for older kids, setting the expectations of which areas your partner will be affecting—and maybe adding some of them slowly before move-in—will help kids and adults adjust to these changes.

Littler kids—preschool and young school age, with daily routines and schedules implemented by leaving the house, but typically fewer activities, less or no homework, and in the age range where they want adult involvement in most play and are learning to be independent when they're home—are simple to deal with but extremely time-consuming for parents. They may still go to bed early and give adults the ability to plan dates "after bedtime," but they require full attention, as they're still in the learning-to-read, aided-learning phase of their educational lives, so even "little homework" is "read with me every day so that I get better at this." Parents have high expectations about how much time and what kind of time they expect to spend with kids in this age range; and while taking time away for ourselves and our social relationships is really essential to coming back with our metaphorical cups full to pour into the relationships with our children, scheduling that becomes challenging.

If you're willing to help each other as parents and partners to take time away from child responsibilities, or to allow additional partners who aren't parenting into the sanctum of family space, rather than feel intruded upon by their presence and help, you can pretty easily be polyamorous in the early years of having kids. If you happen to have easy and flexible kids, they're small and movable. If you have kids who get very wedded to their locations for routine, partners can come to you. (I had one of each kind of child—my son could sleep anywhere and my daughter needed to be in her exact kind of sound and light environment to fall asleep before being laid in her crib, so which parent didn't matter, but home with the blackout curtains and noise machine sure did.)

I expressed in earlier chapters that because phases with them change so rapidly—in terms of needs, development, sleep, and habits—babies and toddlers are both hard and easy polyamorously. There is lots of standing polyamory advice (and social advice in general) about letting people close down into social units upon having babies that in the years since the 2020 lockdowns is getting significantly questioned in public discourse. In the next chapter, I talk about deliberate family building in polyamorous households, and the various issues that can arise and choices that folks can make and have made. There are so many alternatives to resigning ourselves to isolation in small units of the nuclear family as we weather several years of rapidly changing conditions with kids before emerging able to once again socialize.

CHAPTER NINE

More on Polyamorous Parenting

One of the less often discussed aspects of having children in any context is the possibility that overwhelming love will not be your first emotional reaction upon a child's birth—that love will be a choice of care you make every day until the unconditional, deep, foundational, jump-into-traffic-for-that-child feeling has snuck in (or sunk in, or grown in, or crept up the back stairs of your brain while you were asleep) over months. This latter possibility is a much more accepted and acceptable narrative for non-biological parents—step-parents and adoptive parents—and sometimes even for fathers. Bio parents, but especially mothers, are flooded with messaging about "the moment you see your baby you'll know" (or even about sooner than that—sometimes the message is that once we feel movement we'll love our incipient child, for example). While I can say from my own and my friends', polyam and monogamous alike, experiences that the person carrying a child often has the earliest sense that this fetus is a real change that is happening to life in an immediate way, there is no certainty that this comes with sudden and complete, life-changing love.

Some folks are lucky enough to be hit by the full power of bonding hormones in an overwhelming rush in a way that means they overwhelmingly love their tiny human the instant they see them. That is great. But if your experience is instead that it takes a few weeks of making the intentional choice to go through the necessary care steps and motions as love develops, and that the big pit of your stomach, say-it-with-your-whole-chest love kicks in when they first smile, or at a specific finger grab, or some other little moment, I want you to know that this is equally valid. And I want those of you who have the former experience to remember that some of your partners may have the latter, and it does not make them bad parents, or unloving ones.

There is an enormous weight of expectations placed upon all parents, but especially mothers, when new children enter your family. As a polyamorous family, you will likely feel all of these from any extended family you have in your lives, which may mean extra sets of well-meaning but demanding parents, in-laws, aunts, uncles, and more. While it is a wonderful thing to have this kind of support, it can also be deeply overwhelming, and it is one of the jobs of the parents who did not birth the child to take point on fielding the expectations, demands, and requests of these relatives. Do not throw a parent who has just birthed a baby into the position of needing to handle social niceties with any family—even their own. (Depending on their dynamic or the relationship your polycule has to them, maybe especially their own.)

Make some plans ahead of time, and be prepared for them to change. Don't shame new moms for needing support and wanting visit time to be about people who are actually coming to offer help, rather than the kinds of relatives who turn up to hold a baby for an hour and expect to be served. If that's the primary kind of relative you have, expect that the non-birthing parents need to be home and doing that work for those visits. Having multiple families of people who will turn up and offer (sometimes helpful, sometimes not) advice and opinions about how things should be done for your child will be extremely overwhelming, even for the people most practiced at setting boundaries. Help. Be a team.

If you're the parent who takes a few weeks (or until a big, gummy smile manifests, or until they coo while gripping your thumb as you give a bottle, or some other milestone) to have the feeling of "this crying, smelly potato that changed our lives is the baby we love and have been hoping for" really kick in, down in your heart, please, take the time to tell your coparents and partners. They can support you through the weeks or months where you're moving through the work as love builds from below. If you're the birthing parent, depending on what else is going on for you emotionally, you may be going through postpartum depression or postpartum anxiety, and having real social support (rather than just listening to people gush about how you must be gloriously happy at how beautiful this baby is) can be essential to you moving through that to a place of healing.

Planning new kids

Family planning for polyam folks works very much like for monogamous people—you have a series of conversations about whether and when you'd like new children, the person with a uterus who intends to carry a child discontinues birth control and folks begin trying to conceive. Sometimes there are complications and medical intervention is needed.

The aspects that may be different for polyamorous people start with the possibility that there might be more options for who the bio parents will be. I use conditional words because today, many folks have predetermined either because of family medical history, because they already have had biological children, or simply by preference, that they'd rather not be the biological parent of a child, and have taken steps to avoid this. If some folks in your household have already had tubal ligations or vasectomies, they're not going to be the bio parents of new children of your family, even if they will be parents. (While some vasectomies are reversible, it is rare, painful, and expensive, so I'm setting that aside as an option.) Of the remaining household members (which in some families is all of you!) you'll then decide how you want to proceed in terms of trying to have kids.

Some families decide who will carry their child, have them discontinue birth control, and have an equal chance of any of their partners within the household being the bio father of the child. In other situations, where the person trying to conceive has partners with penises outside the household, they use barrier methods with non-household partners and only go barrier-free with a partner with whom they're trying to conceive. The case that came up the least in folks I spoke to, and in the years I've known polyamorous folks in community, is when people live with multiple partners who could get them pregnant but choose to only try to conceive with one of them, using barriers with the others. The folks I spoke to who went this route either chose to do this because someone was intending to get a vasectomy but had not yet, or had plans for children that pre-dated the formation of the household. During the survey data collection, I spoke to one of the men in a quad relationship where one previously existing couple already had children, so when the whole unit considered whether to have more children, the couple who had not yet had children were the ones to "take their turn." They'd always planned to have at least one child together, so this was the culmination of those plans—the child simply has additional parents.

Unplanned children

A common question for folks engaging in polyamorous relationships is "What will you do if there's an unplanned pregnancy?" There are a variety of ways in which this might occur, so let's talk about it.

Sometimes, an unplanned pregnancy is less complicated because there's only one partner who might be the biological father of the child, and it's an expected, nesting or apparently primary partner of the birthing parent. I say that this is less complicated only because the questions become similar to those in a monogamous context. Would the birthing parent like to be a parent? Would the partner with whom they are having a baby like to as well? These are the first questions. If you're nesting with or co-primary with any of the possible fathering partners, the questions become very similar. There are complications, but most of them are not based in your polyamory, they are similar to the complications monogamous folks face. They're about whether you feel emotionally, financially, and physically prepared to have a child. I used "apparently primary" above because even if you're not hierarchical, to external viewers nesting partners often have a certain degree of apparent priority, and for this issue there is a layer of complexity removed for those partners. You don't have to explain who this person is, their relationship to you, or how it's going to change your other relationships to family and friends if you announce a pregnancy in these cases.

That is not to say that unplanned pregnancies are ever uncomplicated, or that the choice of whether one feels prepared to parent is not a major one, or one that a whole relationship or household is necessarily united on. But those issues, despite sometimes involving more potential emotional parents, are relatively similar to the monogamous ones when the physical parents are known.

When the biological parent is uncertain, but between a range of relatively expected, established or nesting partners, it is not that different. You have the same concerns for the birthing parent, and more discussions with the different possible other parents.

Assuming the birthing parent is going forward with the pregnancy, if you want to learn the paternity of the child for medical history reasons, or to simplify birth certificate paperwork and not have to amend a birth certificate later, there are now blood test options for paternity tests available very early in pregnancy. It used to be that prenatal paternity testing was invasive and discouraged, and now it is not so. It might not be covered by your insurance, but as someone who had it (ten years ago, even!) it is not prohibitively expensive, and if the timing of the information is important to you, it is available. Some states require you go through specific laboratories in order for the test to count for legal purposes for the birth certificate in order to override the marital presumption of paternity. In the United Kingdom, similarly, courts now will allow the marital presumption of paternity to be overridden with a DNA test, and since prenatal DNA testing is possible it can be used. Wherever you are, you should confer with a local attorney if you'd like to make sure you are granting legal rights to the appropriate parents via birth certificate and DNA testing choices.

The marital presumption of paternity is a legal shortcut, that is inherited from tradition established in English common law that essentially says that if a woman is married and gives birth to a child, her husband is the legal father of that child. The Uniform Parentage Act of 2002, which many states have adopted or used as a basis for their local parentage laws, includes children born not just within a marriage but also within 300 days after the termination of a marriage. Some states have taken advantage of the lack of clarity around whether this applies to same-sex couples to allow same-sex couples to claim parentage through their marriage regardless of biology, while others have not. In many states there is a time limit or a requirement that you show that it is in the best interest of the child to change who birth certificate parents are, so if it is important to a not-married potential parent that they be acknowledged on a birth certificate, consult a family lawyer in your area, get a paternity test early, and acknowledge paternity appropriately. Some states do allow multiple parents—we will discuss this more fully in Chapter 11, but because mechanisms differ state to state, the most important thing to do if you'd like legal acknowledgement of more than two parents is to seek advice from a lawyer friendly to non-traditional family structures.

In the UK, the legal marital presumption of paternity exists, but can be overridden not just with a DNA test as in the US, but also with simple proof of the mother cohabiting with the alleged father or sworn statements "of the behavior of the couple" at the time the child was conceived. This is partly because UK courts in some countries (notably Scotland) have less power to compel blood testing than their American and Canadian counterparts do. Many people prefer to offer DNA proof to speed up and simplify the parentage process.

When not everyone parents

If not all of the people in the household want to parent, this may be a serious issue. It is very possible to maintain romantic and intimate relationships through a pregnancy and early childhood without parenting together; but it is very hard to live together through the birth of a baby and not do at least some child caretaking. If the non-parent partners are open to being caretaking "aunt"/"uncle" or other important adult figures and occasionally changing a diaper or holding a baby so Mom can grab a shower while Dad is working, that's probably a level-set that's doable; but committing to remain in the home while there will be a newborn present and not parent them if one truly wanted to be child-free, would be an enormous relational strain.

I interviewed two families who had done versions of this.

BABY GREENS

The Green family are a sweet MFF vee triad from Maine who had been living together for five years, changed their last names to legally match, combined many of their finances (though not their retirement plans, which they each managed individually through work), and held a commitment ceremony to celebrate their union with the member of their household to whom they couldn't be legally married when they discovered that they were expecting a child. Margie, the woman expecting this baby, was excited about it, as she'd always wanted to be a mom and this timing was very reasonable for them in terms of their ages and finances (they were all mid-30s and owned their home, and had reasonably established careers—pretty much dream circumstances). James, their partner, got excited and on board with coparenting quickly and was ready with a diaper bag and brain full of dad jokes before the baby's arrival. However, Emily, her platonic nesting partner and meta through James, had always assumed they'd have a child-free life, and this transition was really not one she was prepared to undertake.

The Greens agreed Emily would be "Auntie Emily" and still nest with them but get a little separation from coparenting tasks—taking extra nights with her non-nesting partner, Tim, during the first year of the baby's life, so she could be supportive of James and Margie without taking on a full parenting role. This was stronger in theory than in practice—the effect of Emily getting frequent baby breaks and becoming, effectively, a part-time member of their household and partially de-nesting complicated finances, complicated emotional connections between the members of household (James and Margie felt unsupported; Emily felt unheard; all felt like there was excessive conflict in a time of transition and like they needed therapy they didn't have time for with a new baby, full-time work, and other partners); and other partners stepping up to equivalently entangled relationships as Emily now maintained led to intense conversations about what their previously made commitments meant to them.

While no one "broke up" formally, there was a de-escalation of relationships that accompanied this over about 18 months that led to the Greens no longer stating that they were a nesting unit and instead framing it as Margie and James are a nesting dyad and they have a few partners who part-time stay in their two guest rooms and are "aunts" and "uncles" to their eldest child and an expected younger one. Emily Green lives with Tim three or four nights out of the week now, and stays with her partner Ella once a week. They haven't divorced the legal marriage between Emily and James or undone the commitment ceremony between Margie, Emily, and James; and all of them, together with Tim, Ella, and some of James's partners, are hoping to find a large piece of land (or adjoining smaller lots) to build homes that work better logistically in the future for their complex and entwined schedules.

The version of parenting cohabitation that worked better in my sample who used the term "aunties and uncles" seemed to be one where there had already been some de-escalation in the relationship. Here is an example of one such:

IVAN, LEANNE, BRAD, AND CORA

Ivan and Leanne are polyamorous and share a home with Ivan's coparent Cora, and her partner Brad, and the two children that Ivan and Cora share with a third coparent who doesn't reside with them. When their triad collapsed several years ago, they decided that since they remained on good terms, staying in one house for maximum stability for their kids was a priority for them. Years later, both Ivan and Cora have had other partners become nesting partners, and their kids are happy with the arrangement. Ivan and his partner Leanne had their first baby, and Cora and Brad are "aunt and uncle" to this child, rather than additional parent figures.

What "aunt and uncle" meant for them in this case is that they don't share payments for daycare for this baby, they don't make medical choices for this youngest child, they aren't including the youngest child in switching which parent "has the kid" on specific days—it is up to Ivan and Leanne to get a sitter if they want time off from their youngest, even if Cora and Brad might be that babysitter (especially if they have the older kids that day and are at home). Brad and Cora didn't do night feedings—although they helped with difficult crying evenings and diaper changes during the newborn stage when "all hands on deck" were very helpful. Imagine having your closest sibling, who has also had a child, and doesn't mind taking direction, come to visit after work many days a week. That was the vibe, as they explained it. Now that the baby is a little older (nearly one at time of writing) it is less intensive and thus less intense help is being offered, but still like a helpful set of aunts and uncles they're there to be a set of hands if Dad is at work and Mom needs a shower. Some of Ivan and Leanne's partners have helped out similarly, when they're available—but the convenience of living in the same place, Leanne tells me, cannot be overstated.

The fact that they all know each other so well from years of coparenting means that when there is conflict, they have some idea what to expect—and they were all prepared to support one another and their kids through the transition of having a new baby with school-age children. When, as Leanne put it, "all my worst habits were at an 11 because of hormones and lack of sleep," there was a whole team to back her up in managing the big kids around taking care of the new baby, not just Ivan who also hadn't slept. She said, "Partners, platonic or otherwise, who have slept and show up for you as a sanity check are lifesavers. It's one of the best things about polyamory in pregnancy and postpartum."

Unplanned with secondary or non-nesting partners

Not all non-nesting partners are secondary—but they are not the expected mothers or fathers of your children, and, honestly, they are often who is meant when someone snidely asks "But what if he gets the other girl pregnant?" The implication that someone is a "side chick" and that getting one's side chick pregnant will blow up your home life is what drips from this question.

There is no such thing as foolproof birth control, and there may eventually be failures of it. Two of my favorite children—the eldest son of one of my best friends and my son—were both unplanned pregnancies based on birth control failures in non-nesting polyamorous relationships. (In the same year, even! It's how we met—at a picnic for polyamorous families, where our two families showed up with babies.) Again, as in the monogamous case, the birthing parent has to make the immediate first decision, and then the conversations with partners begin; but in a non-nesting relationship, or a case where the possibility of the baby being from a non-nesting relationship exists, those conversations can be more complicated.

Are folks going to change their living situations to now reside together to care for this baby they've created? Is this why the polyamorous cohabitation is going to happen in the first place? (That's what happened for me.) Are any other relationships in the network going to change? That relational strain we mentioned on any partners who don't want to parent—what if one of those is a current nesting partner of one of the biological parents? Or, conversely, what if the biological parent doesn't want to parent, but another partner of the birthing parent will? These become more complex conversations, and the determination of paternity, of who will be present and supportive for the birthing parent, and of who will be present and supportive and caretaking for the baby all become potentially separate conversations.

If you merge multiple households to accommodate a pregnancy and a baby, that's a move on a deadline. You compress all the concerns of the previous chapters into a few frantic months of make-it-work. Sometimes this means you misjudge things. Or you are trying your absolute hardest to make them work "because you should" to make parenting work, but actually you're all very bad roommates and need to separate again, banging up your relationships in the process.

These are all very general statements because it's hard to give concrete advice—everyone's lives will differ—but let me give you some examples folks were willing to share with me, and the different ways those worked.

I have referenced my family and the vee I lived in throughout the book, but I'd like to get more detailed and share the story of my son's birth and our family building a bit here. I was newly in a relationship with my partner Brian, having moved to Connecticut with my then-husband less than a year prior. I was feeling...off, and took a pregnancy test, which came back positive. My husband and I had a really uncomfortable and unfortunate conversation (It's fine to not want to have kids! It's really rough to have led with "Do they do abortions on Labor Day?" when your partner isn't on that page), and I let Brian know that I was going to see a doctor and likely keep a baby, and maybe likely to be in relational conflict about this. Cut forward a few months, and I was decidedly pregnant, getting divorced, and figuring out plans with Brian and his partner, Megan, for moving into the house that Brian was renovating for himself. Megan had met Brian around the same time I did, and we decided to parent together after all moving in together shortly after the baby was born. The downsides of an unexpected pregnancy were obvious—my marriage didn't survive the transition of one partner not wanting to parent (luckily it turned out that this fault of birth control had happened such that genetics lined up for the partner who did), but on the upside we did manage to turn this into a pretty smooth move-in and series of transitions over the year.

There aren't reliable statistics on how many pregnancies are planned versus unplanned (lots of people like to claim planning for "happy accidents," many people plan carefully for kids, and lots are willing enough to admit that they didn't plan the timing of their children), but the polyamorous folks I know who have had unplanned first children have responded with kindness and community for one another. Folks who didn't choose to move in with one another (as with one respondent to my survey, who moved in with partners with her child several years later) instead coparented in community carefully and creatively.

In our case, we all helped with Brian's renovations so we could get moved into the new house as quickly as possible and so that it would have some aspects of all of our taste in it. We got moved in, acting as a family starting quickly, and the second child in our family was a planned child a couple years later. There were definitely some "rush job" details in our move-in—we didn't really consider if we kept house the same way or what details of housekeeping would look like (like who would cook when or clean when)—we were moving in together to figure out childrearing and we were going to sort out the rest of it as we went. When we eventually split up, there were lots of reasons, but our separate houses being very different from each other's is perhaps a tell we might have noticed if we hadn't jumped to the top of the relationship escalator with family building and decided this meant we had to try to be everything to each other forever.

It doesn't always break down when folks form a family over these unexpected situations, as the following case study shows.

ELLIE, DAN, AND MIKE

Ellie, Dan, and Mike from Los Angeles moved in together while Ellie was expecting their first child 11 years ago, and remain together to this day. Mike and Ellie currently have some non-nesting partners; Dan works a schedule that he says makes it too hard to date. They did paternity testing to know whose medical information applied, but Ellie and Dan got married to simplify house purchasing while she was still pregnant, so he was on the birth certificate as the father even before they found out who the biological dad is, and the family didn't tell me who the father of that child is. Presumption of paternity strikes! All three of them parent equally, and they live in a three-bedroom house with their two kids. (They planned on the second one, two years later.) They acknowledged that moving in quickly had some growing pains, but because they all had similar habits and values, it's worked out in the long run for them. Even if they had a bigger house, Mike told me, they probably wouldn't move any of their other partners in, because they're very used to each other's strengths and weaknesses and making that big a transition again would be too much upheaval—at a minimum until the kids are out of school. "You get used to who picks up and folds blankets at the end of the night and who runs the

> dishwasher and what's worth a reminder and what isn't—a new person would shake it all up and then it's back to figuring out that Dan doesn't do dishes behind himself as he cooks."

Those small details are what make any house into a home—you decide people's foibles are the ones you can live with. As someone who tends to planning (and a neurodivergent person who wants to make the expectations explicit), I've always found that this goes best if folks get a chance to explore their style of living and have some idea of what compromises they'll need to reach going into it. But life is full of growth and surprises; none of us are the same person forever, and love is dedicating to supporting each other's growth.

CHAPTER TEN
Breakdown—Cohabitation

Not all growth is growing together. Sometimes, the pattern means that partners grow apart. When folks decide they can't live together any longer, or they can't date any longer while cohabiting, it's a complicated situation. In monogamous relationships, if we decide that we aren't going to be with someone anymore (even if the cost of rent means we're going to take a couple months to move), that's generally pretty firmly and strongly a breakup, and it's well understood that we aren't going to be in close contact anymore. Our future relationships may even think it's a red flag if we stay in contact at all, if it isn't someone we share children with. Whereas in the polyamorous community, there are breakups, but there is also the option of transformations and de-escalation of relationships.

De-escalation

The polyamorous community at large talks a fair bit about de-escalating relationships and how the option to change your relationship into a different form if it isn't working in its present incarnation is one of the strengths of polyamorous relating.

I think this is true. But it's true because in relating polyamorously, in being within a larger network and taking the time to look at the interrelationship of our connections and how they affect us and one another, and in actually addressing our needs, wants, and boundaries in the commitments we make, we're taking apart normative assumptions about relationships. So, if you're choosing to engage in a couple of very relationship-escalator-driven relationships at once and the only norm you've questioned is that more than one is allowed, de-escalation may not be something that feels reasonable or natural for you. (Even if you've questioned all the assumptions, it might not feel natural—it might just feel like another thing you're questioning, and that's okay.)

So what is a de-escalation?

There are as many answers to this as there are relationships, because a de-escalation is when you stay in relationship or contact with someone who you previously had one form of intimate relationship with, but remove some aspect of that relationship. The most common form we see in polyamorous networks is moving from lovers to friends, but you could also have:

- partners to coparents
- partners to roommates
- romantic and sexual partners to only sexual partners or friends with benefits
- no longer having a kink dynamic on top of a friendship or a sexual or romantic relationship, and redefining the boundaries there

- living together to not living together, maintaining the emotional and sexual relationship but changing logistics
- other logistical changes that feel like a significant downshift to the people involved
- a divorce, whether or not the people involved stay emotionally or physically involved (some people divorce to "uncouple" and gain greater autonomy/reduce couple's privilege, for example)
- removing the sexual aspect of a relationship but maintaining the emotional aspects
- and more—remember the key is just "you downshift one or more areas but not all."

De-escalations are sometimes necessary, as children of divorce (or polyamorous coparents who aren't with all their parenting partners) will tell you—some life situations require staying in contact with people after a romantic or sexual aspect of a relationship ends. Or if you have entangled friend groups, sometimes it's just a reality that you will be in contact in ways that involve not having a drawn-out period of no contact or a typical monogamous-script period of "everybody hates each other" for a while. And sometimes you consciously choose to avoid that because it's just that one part of a relationship isn't working and you don't want to throw the baby out with the bathwater. Making that conscious choice is the one polyamorous people most often tout as an "evolved" or "mature" way to behave and that monogamy really doesn't have a script for. (Monogamous culture doesn't like, but understands, needing to get along with your kid's other parent—even if it equally makes room for or encourages hating their guts as opposed to being on a team—and managing to hang out in a group instead of forcing your friends to take sides in a breakup is picking up steam all over, it seems. But choosing to stay 1:1 friends? Choosing to remain emotionally close? Or roommates? Or to decide that being sexually incompatible doesn't end your marriage? Monogamy doesn't really have scripts for any of those.)

Why do scripts matter?

The reason I keep talking about these scripts, the reason they matter, is because we don't just default to them when we don't know what to do, but often we build our sense of "what to do" and our list of wants around them without noticing. Cultural messages around "how relationships are" and "how relationships end" are something we have to decide if we buy into them or not within a polyamorous context. In a monogamous context, the basic assumption is that you will try to ride the relationship escalator all the way up with your partner, and when/if you don't, if the relationship "fails," that you will cut that person completely out of your life. We see this in the way folks talk about people who are friends with their exes with an implication that they must still be involved or trying to get back together, or when people suggest that at any difficulty in re-evaluating boundaries with an ex, you should just stop seeing them. While I think some people can use a little bit of distance before trying to determine the boundaries of a new friendship after the end of a romance, in particular, I don't think any of these are requirements—just cultural assumptions.

If we're ditching the scripts, we're building relationships where we customize our commitments with and boundaries regarding individuals. We allow each of our friendships, loves, and connections to be as unique as the people we're in them with. This requires more communication than checking a box marked "friend" and only doing friend things as we expect others around us perceive them, or riding up the escalator together.

Why is polyamory good at de-escalations?

Polyamorous relationships, especially non-hierarchical polyamorous relationships and relationship-anarchist-style relationships, already question these paradigms, don't ride the whole escalator typically, have included questions about the "Whys" behind relationship choices, and in being pick-and-choose about commitments can often have space for flexibility. So, if we're already saying we're girlfriends who love each other deeply and have sex, but don't intend to move in together, adding or removing a kink dynamic might be a very significant change that requires serious negotiation and feels like a Big Step up or down an escalator or stairway—but we're pretty well equipped for those negotiations. Or if we've already had massive relationship change by opening up a formerly monogamous relationship, we know what these skills are. We have co-created a new relationship and determined our boundaries in a new space with new conditions and additional circumstances.

But, just like with opening up, de-escalating can be very vulnerable and difficult. It's not a walk in the park or intellectual decision of "I want to do this and now my emotions, guts, and nervous system are all completely on board with my brain." The regulation lag of knowing you want to do something and having it still be hard, because determining where your new boundaries are often involves overstepping them unintentionally (on your part and your partner's!) is very real and the feeling of grief that accompanies a breakup can sometimes seem misplaced in a de-escalation—so we beat ourselves up for "still being so upset" about someone who is still in our life when we aren't grieving the person, we're grieving a role or a thing we imagined about that relationship.

So, what can we do about it?

Unfortunately, we're human and these are relationships, so mostly, we can do the following:

- Be thoughtful about what we want to keep from our relationships and proactive about positive interactions that lead to that.
- Have a care for our own and our partners' boundaries and where they come from—How does our trauma play together in conflict? Have we de-escalated to avoid an area where our responses to stimuli were triggering for one another? What can we do to support each other in our new relationship?
- Be gentle with ourselves if it's still hard—because sometimes it will be.
- Remember that picking the off-escalator, off-script option is always available and should always be considered before making a decision, but is not always better. We can decide that a particular de-escalation is too hard and we need to peel more layers away or stop seeing each other.

Personally, I try to de-escalate to a place of friendship, because I'm not good at going from "all the romance and sex and entanglement" to nothing, but also not good at landing in a place in the middle. Saying "let's keep everything the same except we won't have sex anymore" sounds awful to me—but I know many people for whom that kind of de-escalation was exactly what their relationship needed. I will say that de-escalating from partners to roommates and coparents, and then later to coparenting in different households with my kids' dad remains one of the harder but more worthwhile series of relationship transitions I've ever gone through, and while I would not underestimate the difficulty of these major life changes, I also would not understate the benefit of getting to a place where everyone is relating as authentically as possible.

Let's talk de-nesting

De-nesting is a style of de-escalation wherein folks who previously lived together decide to no longer do so. It's usually the term used for this when people are keeping the relationship otherwise intact.

ABBIE, TOM, AND ROB

Abbie, Tom, and Rob moved into Rob's three-bedroom home in upstate New York in 2019. They're a triad but have very independent, dyadic relationships between one another. Each of them had their own room, and liked it that way, because they had relationships outside the house as well. However, Abbie explained that it felt, over the year and a half that she lived there, that she only half moved in, because Rob had the public rooms of the house furnished, and arranged in a particular way, so her things were stuffed into her bedroom, or felt like they were intruding into spaces that were already meant for other purposes in the living and dining room. "Tom kind of felt the same way, but Tom's more of a vocal fighter than I am, so Tom made a fuss and demanded a section of room for a desk and they'd get in awful fights about Tom then still making messes outside his new section of living room." This situation only got worse once there were pandemic lockdowns. "I was an essential worker and they weren't and the

> whole thing got unmanageable. We maybe could have figured it out if I hadn't been in this kind of stress and they hadn't been locked in with each other stewing on their issues."
>
> In order to save the romantic relationships, Abbie decided to move out before things got more tense. She moved into her own apartment alone, and a couple years later is still with both of them, and they with each other. She says it wasn't easy and that it took a significant amount of negotiation and practice at following through for one another on new promises and commitments to show that they really were committed to growing together, just not in a home together. So many cultural scripts put living together up at the top of things, along with marriage, that for those in non-traditional relationships or who aren't able to marry all their partners, the move out can feel overwhelming and like a failure.

A de-nesting might be differently emotional than this. Remember Michelle, who moved out from the quad and moved in with her other partner to have a child (Chapter 2)? That de-nesting was bittersweet, because it involved some relationships realizing they had truly hit a ceiling and weren't going to meet someone's needs dissolving, but the relationship that survived the transition was all the richer for the changes, and she's really happy in both her relationships and as a parent.

Staying in the nest after a breakup

On the opposite side of the coin, the breakup where for logistical reasons folks stay nested for some period has some monogamous equivalent. We have all seen or heard of someone who needed to stay living somewhere while they sorted out who's keeping a place and how, or where the other person (in this case maybe people) will go. To avoid prolonging an unintended period like this, my (maybe unromantic but practical) advice is to plan for the possibility of something going wrong in your home situation. Talk out what happens if folks break up. Have a rainy day fund for if the landlord sells out from under you. Have "fuck you money"—the amount needed to quit everything and restart for a couple months if something goes entirely wrong.

I don't mean that we all need to have our finances perfectly in order to be polyamorous and move in together, but to best avoid situations where we're living together out of obligation (or the "Monogamy? In this economy??" joke brought to horrible life) and instead get to be as authentic as possible, not extending ourselves to the point where there are no savings, or including in our household budget an item for savings until there are six months of the full household expenses, and agreeing with all adults that if there's a breakup, it gets split evenly all ways to cover moving and housing costs so that folks have the option to move if they choose to.

You can also make family or household-level plans for what happens if something goes wrong with your situation—like the landlord selling the house that we mentioned above, or needing to move urgently; or "if there are relationship problems, we'll go to therapy before they're breakups, to try to resolve things, and then we'll tap into the rainy day savings if we break up for moving costs." These plans are generally plans, not agreements or promises. The one agreement I'd suggest folks include is if there are any shared funds they intend to divide, get on an agreement-level same page about it; if you can't, save separately. Viewing the possibility of a breakup, and its attendant complications, as a game you're on a team together for, is way more effective than fighting each other. Doing some early planning before there is conflict positions you better to support each other to comfortably transition through relationship transformations and breakups than waiting until emotions are high enough to require those breakups.

Leases, sales, and messy breakups

Polyamorous people are not immune to the possibility of the messy breakup and so it is up to folks who are getting into housing situations to balance what makes sense for them in terms of leases and ownership. We talked in earlier chapters about the practicalities of these—how some people were able to have all their partners on leases and titles and mortgages, but others encountered significant barriers—but the question for consideration is in fact what works as a balance for your relationship. Is it better to have the equity of being a part owner of a house, or the documentary evidence and credit effect of having your name on a lease, or is it better to have an easier time separating your affairs again in case of a split? These are questions that individuals have to answer for themselves, but it's worth considering how much the "exit plan" is complicated in each case.

Regardless of how your exit plan works, please consider seeking both polyamory-friendly therapy and community in the aftermath of a breakup, if you were not engaged with either of them before. In seeking a polyamory-affirming therapist, do not be afraid to ask specific questions, to inform them of the broad strokes of your situation if you're asking questions by email or contact form, and don't be embarrassed. You are hiring someone to help you. This is a field that is growing, but that has fewer informed professionals than there is need for, currently, and checking if someone fits your needs and situation is you being a smart patient.

Protecting assets

One attorney I spoke to (mostly about custody issues polyamorous families face) mentioned that monogamous families benefit from the presumption that all of their relationships could have been forever and it's a fluke that theirs wasn't; polyamorous families are working uphill against the opposite. We often aren't recognized as families because we can't use marriage as our mechanism to unite all our relationships, so we're using workarounds to approximate the protections for ourselves that monogamous marriages generate for participants in them.

One of these areas is how to make sure inheritance and homes or other assets are protected. There was a lot of talk on Reddit about ten years ago among polyamorous folks suggesting to one another that if they had a hard time buying property together, they could form an LLC and have the LLC do so. This only works in some states, but check with an attorney to see if it's viable for you! In addition to making sure that you get a will in order, putting jointly held (or owned by one person but intended to be managed or passed to another) homes or accounts in trust with the help of a local lawyer can secure these to a greater degree. Talk with local counsel, but trusts or irrevocable trusts can be a way to secure property in states where making them the property of an LLC and all polycule members co-owners of the LLC doesn't work. This all is also protective for members of the LGBTQ community, because in light of the *Dobbs* decision, it seems likely that marriage rights in the US will contract further.[1]

1 *Dobbs* v. *Jackson Women's Health Organization* is a 2022 US Supreme Court decision that reversed the right to abortion federally by overturning the presumption of a right to privacy determined under *Roe* v. *Wade*; the concurrences include justices suggesting that cases involving the right to contraception, gay marriage, and other rights be examined and dismissed as well.

CHAPTER ELEVEN

Breakdown—Coparenting

When coparenting or child-involved relationships break down, there are some considerations that folks frequently ask questions about or have concerns around. These are the tiny seeds of real concern that make polyamorous people allow "What about the children?" conversations to go on for too long—because we worry about the what-ifs of what it will mean for our kids if our relationships break down, or if our chosen coparents aren't as reliable as we hope they will be in the long term and we de-escalate them out of those roles.

Honestly, what that means for polyamorous families is the same thing it means for monogamous families—that we have to be sincere and serious in our partner selection, that parenting compatibility is a separate consideration from romantic compatibility and should be considered on its own, and that our kids deserve the care and consideration of us taking the time to worry about those issues before deeply entangling someone in their lives, not after. (Yes, I am a "polyamorous parents who seek coparents should date like divorced parents who seek coparents—cautiously" person. This is not always a popular viewpoint.) I do think that polyamory and the general sense of being able to share these concerns and considerations with a greater number of people can free us from the feeling that we are "stuck" in a phase where our kids control our dating futures—not everyone needs to be auditioning for the role of coparent in our polyamory and not everyone needs to ride the relationship escalator in that way, and this is very freeing, but not everyone agrees with this take either. That said, breakups do affect our children, especially when they are with people who have become a part of their lives—so let's talk about it.

Legal coparents and coparenting agreements

The very first stop on this ride of talking about breakups is whether this is the kind of breakup that generally signifies needing legal paperwork to formalize the shared parenting you'll continue to do. If you're both or all parents on a child's birth certificate and plan to live separately, you should probably get a coparenting agreement written down and formalized by a family court in your jurisdiction. It'll lay out requirements for paying support (in most states, this is determined by a formula that takes into account how much each of you makes, what other children you have, and the percentage of the time spent by the kid(s) at each home), the amount and schedule of time kids will spend in each home as a default (you can always deviate by agreement, but a written agreement gives you a default to fall back to), a plan for who will pay for expenses or how they'll be split, and who will claim the child on taxes, as well as maybe other details. (Some folks include holiday schedules, details of how far apart the parents can live from one another, what school the children will attend, who will fund higher education, what notice parents will give each other about changes to the child's other household, and more.) In a more straightforward case like where two folks are already the legal parents of the children, paperwork can be done yourselves with assistance of court family services or with the help of a lawyer; if you have three+ legal parents you probably already have a family lawyer or two, but if not, everyone will probably want one to advise them on the coparenting agreement.

In the UK, as in the US, if you agree to terms for your children's coparenting agreement, it should be relatively straightforward to have it approved by the court; however, in cases where your life is outside of norms, the advocates I spoke to recommended you work with someone local specialized in family law to make sure you are not submitting to a court who will decide that your relationships are not in the best interest of your children. The best interest standard that family courts use is subjective—there is common law case law that helps support it as a standard but judges are allowed significant interpretational latitude, and doing your best to make your agreements when you're all in agreement so that your plans are rapidly reviewed and rubber-stamped, not heard as a conflicted court case, can matter; as well as conferring with legal professionals to do your best to be heard in as friendly a court as possible (if two parents reside in homes in slightly different jurisdictions, picking which one to file in can make a difference).

If you're not both or all legal parents but have been acting as a parent to a child for a long period of time, up to the child's entire life, you can speak to a family lawyer in your area about whether applying for the same kind of parenting agreement is available to you as a "psychological parent" of that child, or whether visitation agreements come under some other statute (statutes intended for grandparents or aunts and uncles who caretake are often applied to step-parents and partners of parents who have breakups but are found to have relationships that it is in the best interests of children to continue). In some states this will mean you get less time with children or limited rights, because you are not considered a full parent, and in others you may simply need to prove the best interest of the child is served or (in the case of an older child) have them state they are interested in maintaining their familial relationship with you. You'd again have this agreement in writing certified by a family court in your area once lawyers helped you and your coparent ex use the appropriate law to draft it.

I mentioned, briefly, the idea of shopping for a therapist in the last chapter, and I want to iterate that a step further and remind you that you get to shop for a lawyer. It is almost always in your better interest to engage someone who works in your local courts and with the judges who will be certifying your agreement, because they'll have a good idea of what is not just legal but also reasonable with that judge and in that venue. Call and, without giving any personal information (like your name or address), give the secretary the broadest strokes of your situation and ask if it's in the attorney's practice scope. They'll tell you if it isn't. Attorneys don't want to take on things that are wildly outside their scope, and will be clear if they've worked with queer families but not polyfamilies or step-parent adoptions and are planning to transfer the knowledge.

Extra-legal agreements

Sometimes, making the legal agreement isn't worth it. You haven't been coparenting for a particularly long time, or the child in question is very young and won't have a clear memory of the situation (if any), or you'll still be living in the same home and all you want is to smooth the de-escalation of your relationship. Each of those scenarios gets a slightly different treatment, with the only similarity being that they're all extra-legal.

Let's address the last one first. If you'd usually make a legal coparenting agreement, but you're staying in the same home and just moving bedrooms or not having date nights or changing "shifts" of coparenting nights to cover each other's nights, you're probably on good enough terms to decide that between yourselves or with a family therapist's help.

I can't recommend enough finding a good, inclusive family therapist or non-monogamy-focused coach who is familiar with the issues of cohabitation and parenting. You can find some links at the end of this book to (non-exhaustive) lists of non-monogamy-aware therapists. Emailing therapists you're hoping to work with and just asking if they feel like your situation or issues are ones they can work with is really the best way to find a good match. People do not try to take on things that are terrible matches for them—it's not in their best interests to get bad results or have frustrating session after frustrating session. Being straightforward that you are polyamorous and that you're going through a major life transition and need support around negotiating changes in schedules and changes in how household tasks are going to be handled if you aren't together but are staying in the same space is the best way to find someone who is willing to help you meet that goal rather than encourage you to immediately move out or insist that the polyamory was the problem here, or some other unhelpful stereotype.

I lived this scenario for almost two years of the time that I cohabited, and parts of it were very functional and parts of it really didn't work for us—which is why I eventually transitioned to living elsewhere and getting a legal custody agreement, etc. It is very hard to "turn off" regardless of whether it is your time to be on duty when you're in the house with kids, especially if they're young kids. If part of what you're hoping to get out of coparenting after a breakup is equitable division of labor, being physically in separate spaces will probably be needed to set new expectations around who a default parent is and when. It is actually much easier, emotionally, to show up as a whole person and reflect on the things you're learning in return from your kids when you only have them part-time. Our culture really doesn't want us to say that—it's supposed to be a major problem to admit that we need time away from them to process and to show up our best, but we absolutely do, and all parents show up better when we get real time off. You don't necessarily need to be in separate physical space for that, but you need better boundaries than I personally had when we were all in one home, in order to create time to do that processing.

De-escalation from coparenting

What if you're not coparenting anymore but you're still relating? It's the opposite of that scenario I lived above, but it's also a situation that requires delicate but extra-legal handling. I mentioned in the chapters about parenting in general that there should have been some discussion of what happens in a breakup from a non-nesting partner if you have kids—this kind of follows a similar pattern. You should be backing down slowly instead of overnight no longer having a connection to a kid. If a de-escalation is happening because of an impending major life change—like a partner becoming long-distance (there is an example below, from one of our study participants)—making the transition as gradual and intentional as possible, and explaining steps as you know them at an age-appropriate level so that kids know what's going on is your best bet for a smooth transition.

When you have lead time, being able to explain that this person loves the child very much and will always be an important person but is moving and isn't going to live with [parent figures] and make parenting choices for [kiddo] anymore, so over the next few months they're going to do more fun things and less serious things, and go to fewer school/doctor-type meetings but still take you to the aquarium like they said, sets expectations appropriately, if you're talking to a preschool/young school-age kid. If you're talking with an older kid, who can better understand the idea of someone getting a job opportunity and moving across country for it and coming back to visit, and might want occasional phone calls from a supportive adult in their life, you can make them a collaborative part of building the transition. Tweens and teens are pretty well able to define their own wants out of these relationships, and while adults of course will arrive with what they're able to offer, kids will also show up with interests and expectations that might be higher or lower that we as their adults will do our best to meet.

If the transition is local (or still resident)—someone has realized they aren't ready to parent or took on too much entwinement and responsibility in coming to be a parental figure in a relationship that is only part of their relationship network, for example—it can be more complicated. In Chapter 9 we talked about the Green family and how they de-nested following one of their family members deciding that being in an aunt role was more appropriate for her level of interest in kids than coparenting. There is a significant chance that someone de-escalating from a parenting role leads to a de-nesting. I have not encountered, in the 17 years I've been polyamorous, someone who de-escalated from parenting and remained nested for the long term with those partners.

Dr. Sheff's (2020) longitudinal study of polyamorous families found that the key to maintaining children's relationships with de-nested ex-partners (who in monogamous land would have become former step-parents with limited if any connection to those kids), was polyaffective connections. Ex-metamours managing the relationship and timing so that kids don't lose relationships is really powerful. When someone maybe doesn't want to spend time with their ex, or take the kids to go for a hike with them or to the museum together, the former metamours who are still friendly enough to have that connection (or at a minimum hand off kids kindly at the start and end of an afternoon) can keep visits up and keep someone present in children's lives.

Coming and going

We've talked a lot about situations in which folks move all together or a partner into a house with kids, but what if kids move into an otherwise existing household? Most of the time, all the previous concerns from this book apply. But there can be one additional complication. The possibility of custody challenges appears. These are the most common legal problems that face polyamorous folks—non-polyamorous coparents or grandparents raising custody challenges based on disapproval of our lives and relationships. They are the most common, but this is not to say that it happens to everyone—people know best who it is that they coparent with and are related to, and whether those people are litigious.

The reality of how negatively a frivolous custody case or frivolous claim to child services will affect a family is determined by the number of marginalizations that magnify the impact. If polyamory is the only way in which you are a member of a marginalized group, and you are relatively well off, white, and Christian or non-religious in the US, you have less to worry about. Not nothing—a dedicated ex or family member can bring up anything there may be in your behavior past and present that could work against you for custody—but if essentially the argument is "polyamory is weird" and you show up good on paper aside from that, in many jurisdictions it will not be nearly as big an issue as it was several years ago. When there are multiple marginalizations, the impacts of prejudice amplify the likelihood that stigma and discrimination have tangible effects. So a person who is BIPOC (Black Indigenous People (Person) of

Color), trans, gay, or visibly disabled is more likely to have negative outcomes when someone brings a frivolous claim about how they are parenting or says they should lose a portion of parenting time because of polyamory. In some jurisdictions, while proceedings are ongoing, custody and visitation can be paused or reduced to supervised visits, and people and their relationships with their children can really suffer in these situations.

When kids are able to move in, having space ready for them, and having folks who live in the house ready to treat them like they're welcome and not like a strange sidecar to a partner is important. This is not just a legal concern (having appropriate space for kids is often a legal requirement) but also a practical and emotional one. When there's been a struggle with custody, partners and children often don't build the kind of emotional rapport that you get in a slow build up to a move in, because parents are being careful and protective of their kid time and crossing every t and dotting every i. So more effort needs to take place after the move to build and rebuild those polyaffective bonds.

PAULA, STEVE, AND ANGIE

Paula is a polyamorous woman from New Hampshire with three kids. Her kids have two different dads, an ex-spouse from a monogamous marriage, and the man she discovered polyamory with a decade ago, who is also now an ex. She doesn't strictly define herself by any style of polyamory but was living in a style some might define as solo-polyamorous for a couple of years with her kids, until she got deeply involved with a couple, Steve and Angie, who invited her and the kids to move into their home. This seemed like a great situation, but the grandparents of her two kids from the ex-spouse challenged the custody situation, claiming that her polyamorous life with Steve and Angie made her an unfit parent.

> She spent a full year fighting to keep custody of the children, and, although she won, that was a year during which she only got supervised visits, not the real time with the kids she was accustomed to. Steve and Angie have gotten to know the girls and built those connections now, but the first couple months after they moved in, where mom and one sibling were really close and settled in and they were not, were a huge transition and really hard on the family.

This is much less common, even for folks with exes who don't get along, than just people being kind of rude ever is—but because it does happen, and because polyamory is not a protected group outside of one town in Massachusetts, it is worth emphasizing.

In 17 years of being polyamorous, I think I've seen people "do polyamory" every possible way. It has always been a smaller subset of people who were willing to do the logistical and communication legwork to live in homes with three or more adults who are romantically or sexually entangled; but as time goes on, I have met more and more of them. When I became a polyamorous parent, I set out to meet other polyamorous parents and discovered that there's an entire subset of our community who took the idea of always outnumbering the children very literally, and even as I'm now a solo-polyamorous coparent, I'm glad for those years of experience living in a vee. This book grew out of curiosity about whether my local anec-data and the folks I was meeting via my coaching practice reflected the reality of how folks live together. (Mostly yes, although maybe I don't know enough triads.)

The legal and logistical challenges to parenting outside the norm are enormous, and my local polyamorous parenting community is amazing. I am so grateful to the people (who I never saw again) who hosted one meetup at East Rock Park where I took the phone numbers of the other polyamorous people with infants and toddlers in 2014. When we're all redefining what the family is in real time, despite zoning regulations, stigma, and the crushing weight of capitalism, it's important to have friends to call who will understand that today, the biggest problem is actually that the kids won't pick up their towels and no other parents have mentioned it all week! ...But I digress.

Whether we're living in walk-up apartments or suburban houses, polyamorous folks are negotiating how to meet our needs for space, conduct relationships in the space where our boundaries overlap, and making adjustments to the furniture and our behavior as needed to support each other's growth for years to come.

APPENDIX

The Interviewees[1]

Chapter 2: The Power of Three

Maggie, Alex, and Amy: Triad who nested and then moved out, from Pennsylvania. I spoke with Maggie.

Keisha, Evan, Michelle, and Devon: Brooklyn quad that moved to a triad plus one relationship off it into a wing of their polycule.

Chapter 3: "But Where Do You All Sleep?"

Ethan, Jennifer, and Melissa: Chicago triad of late-20s people.

Josh and household: Large polyam household in Massachusetts who have one roommate and several polycule members. I spoke with Josh about their evolution over eight years.

Amanda, Ben, and Susan: Portland, Oregon vee, formerly a triad. I spoke with Amanda.

Eva: member of a triad in the northeast I spoke to in follow-ups.

Chapter 4: "I Could Never Do That"

Josh, Jonah, and Debbie: A triad from California. I emailed with Jonah.

1 Names have been changed to ensure anonymity.

Mary: A member of a complicated constellation, nesting in a vee in NYC.

Chapter 5: Making It Your Own

Daniel, Charles, and Mark: A gay triad from San Francisco. I spoke with Daniel after emailing.

Nicole, Matt, and John: A vee from Texas. I interviewed Nicole.

Lynn, member of a complex polycule who nests with two partners. Did a video call with me to show me their home.

Chapter 6: That's So Meta

Marcus: I interviewed Marcus, 41, part of an male-female-male vee from Atlanta, about their household.

Sean: Late 30s, lives in a female-male-female triad household with a young child and some outside partners that complete their polycule. He asked to be identified as from "a midwestern city."

Chapter 7: All About Money

Mark, Cynthia, Dave, and Alice: A quad from California who I spoke to one representative of after he answered the survey. All four individuals are in their 30s, they have five children between them who cohabited with them for the period we discuss in the book.

Britney, Liza, and Jane: A triad from Seattle and then Arizona; I spoke with Jane about their three years of cohabitation in an apartment and then a subsequent move to a home Jane inherited.

Chapters 8 & 9: Polyamorous Parenting

Margie, Emily, and James: Maine triad with non-nesting

relationships. Emily is "aunt" to the baby the other two had but is legal spouse of James.

Ivan, Cora, and Jean: Triad from Connecticut who coparent, broke up in 2018, legal three-parent custody agreement. Now (2022 interview) Cora and Ivan are not together but nest and live in a shared home with some of their partners, Leanne and Brad, and each have non-nesting partners. Jean is now in a monogamous relationship with a spouse. I spoke with Cora, Ivan, and Leanne (2x).

Dave, Emma, and Jason: Triad from New Jersey, two kids 12 and 10, pandemic house changes. I spoke with Emma.

Jenna, Rich, Amy, and Larry: Emails from Jenny and Larry, phone call with Jenna—older teen children, living in a quad after they broke up, struggles coming out to kids.

Mike, Dan, and Ellie: Triad who moved in together along with the birth of their first child 11 years ago. Two follow-up conversations with Mike.

Shana and Joe: From outside of Boston, MA. I emailed with both Shana (39) and Joe (44) and spoke with Joe on the telephone, regarding their "complex intertwined network of relationships," including nesting with Reggie (40) and their several children from previous relationships.

Chapter 10 & 11: Breakdown

Abbie, Tom, and Rob: Upstate New York triad where one person moved out to sustain the relationships.

Keisha, Evan, and Michelle, Devon from Chapter 2.

Paula, Steve, and Angie: From New Hampshire. I spoke with Paula about her custody battle.

Glossary

So we're on the same page with vocabulary!

Polyamory: A subset of consensual non-monogamy where the assumption is that all partners may seek out multiple loving relationships. From the Greek *poly*, meaning many, and Latin *amor*, meaning love. Structures beyond this vary between people and groups of people.

Chosen family: Exactly as the name states, people one chooses to be one's family in place of blood family, because of shared values and emotional support.

Compersion: Happiness at the joy of one's partner in another relationship; sometimes referred to as the opposite of jealousy.

Consensual non-monogamy: An umbrella term for relationships in which all partners have explicit agreements to engage in romantic, intimate, and/or sexual relationships with multiple people. Depending on what these agreements are, they can be a variety of different types or styles of relationship, such as polyamory, swinging, monogamish relationships, or other terms that the folks involved agree upon. All of these communities fall under the umbrella of consensual non-monogamy.

Dyad: A relationship of two people; can be monogamous or the relationship between any two people in a polyamorous network.

Hierarchical: Refers to relationships or networks in which certain partnerships are prioritized above others and/or given additional powers in rule-setting. Often, but not always, the early result of people discovering polyamory when they have an existing partnership.

Hinge: The shared partner between two people—so called because in using shapes to describe *polycules*, they're often the point a shape hinges on; also because hinges can open and close, as a convenient metaphor for describing the relationship between *metamours*.

Kitchen table polyamory: A style of polyamorous relationship in which the interrelationship of a network, and the integration of multiple romantic relationships into one life or group, is prioritized. Close relationships between metamours and/or telemours are strongly encouraged or required. The name comes from the notion that all members of a network "can sit around the kitchen table in their PJs, drinking coffee" (Kimchi Cuddles #452: https://kimchicuddles.com).

Metamour: The partner of one's partner; from the root *meta*, beyond—so literally "beyond love." Often abbreviated to meta.

New relationship energy: The excitement and giddiness that comes with a new relationship and its early stages; some scientists believe it is the result of oxytocin and vasopressin. It is potentially obsessive and similar to limerence, except that it occurs after a relationship has begun. It can be extremely positive, but also for some people jittery and challenging. Often abbreviated to NRE.

Non-hierarchical: Refers to relationships or networks which strive for equal autonomy and standing of relationships rather than prioritizing one over another. These are not immune from "inherent hierarchy," such as shared responsibilities with a partner with whom one shares children or a home, or with whom one has been for a much longer time, but they ascribe to an ideal of involving all network members in discussions of rule changes that will impact them, and limiting prioritization when possible.

Parallel polyamory: A style of polyamorous relationship in which each individual relationship exists largely independent of either partner's additional romantic or sexual relationships, and in which there is not an intentional focus on entwining the relationship network. There may be close relationships between some metamours or telemours, but there is no requirement for this and there may be low or no contact between some members of the larger relationship network.

Polyaffective relationship: A term coined by the researcher Dr. Elisabeth Sheff for caring relationships that would not exist without a polyamorous connection—as connections between metamours, or the love for a child who is not legally or biologically your own but connected by relationships, not just by that polyamorous parent figure but their extended family—these extra grandparents, aunts, and uncles are polyaffective bonds.

Polycule: A network of interconnected relationships; can be used to refer to the network itself, or a chart illustrating the same. A portmanteau of *poly* and *molecule,* because of the varied possible configurations and how they can resemble charts of the chemical structures of molecules. Groups and networks larger than four people often simply use "polycule" or "constellation" to describe their network, rather than using one of the specialized terms for smaller units, as the shapes can get complicated.

Primary relationship/partner: The prioritized relationship or partner in a hierarchical set-up. Some people have multiple primary partners, or leave the option for additional primary-level relationships to exist; but many who prefer this relationship structure do not.

Quad: A four-person relationship network where all the parties are romantically interconnected.

Secondary relationship/partner: Additional partners or relationships beyond the primary ones in a hierarchical network. They often have to accept pre-existing rules or limits on time defined by the primary relationship members, without recourse to changing these.

Solo polyamory: A form of polyamory in which an individual chooses to be their own "primary partner," building connections without the assumption of progressing up the "relationship escalator" with one or more. Often includes the assumption of living apart from all partners.

Telemour: The partner of a metamour who is not your shared partner; from the root *tele,* distant—so literally "distant love." Used less commonly than metamour.

Triad: A relationship of three people, all of whom are romantically involved with one another. A triad contains three dyads (A and B; A and C; and B and C) as well as the triad relationship (A and B and C). One of the most publicized forms of polyamory in mainstream media.

V: A relationship network including three people where there are two "ends" who are metamours but not romantically involved with one another, and a hinge partner. A V (sometimes written vee) polycule contains two dyads (A with B and B with C).

Resources

Books

The Polyamorists Next Door, Elisabeth Sheff, 2014

The Polyamorous Home, Jess Mahler, 2017

The Polyamorous Pregnancy, Jess Burde, 2013

Polyamory and Parenthood: Navigating Non-Monogamy as Parents of Young Children, Jessica and Joseph Daylover, 2023

Polyamory Breakup Book, Kathy Labriola, 2019

Relationship Anarchy, Juan-Carlos Perez-Cortes, 2022

PolySecure, Jessica Fern, 2020

NonViolent Communication, Marshall Rosenberg, 2019

Mom Rage, Minna Dubin, 2023

How Many Grown Ups Do You Have? A Book About Unconventional Families, Polina Buchan, 2023

Therapy links

www.polyfriendly.org

www.kapprofessionals.org

References

Hamilton, J.E. (2019) *A Phenomenological Exploration of Jealousy's Archetypal Nature in Polyamorous Individuals* [Doctoral dissertation, Pacifica Graduate Institute]. ProQuest Dissertations & Theses Global.

Haupert, M.L., Gesselman, A.N., Moors, A.C., Fisher, H.E., and Garcia, J.R. (2017) "Prevalence of experiences with consensual nonmonogamous relationships: Findings from two national samples of single Americans." *Journal of Sex & Marital Therapy* 43, 5, 424–440.

Matsick, J.L., Conley, T.D., Ziegler, A., Moors, A.C., and Rubin, J.D. (2014) "Love and sex: Polyamorous relationships are perceived more favourably than swinging and open relationships." *Psychology & Sexuality* 5, 4, 339–348.

Moors, A.C., Gesselman, A.N., and Garcia, J.R. (2021) "Desire, familiarity, and engagement in polyamory: Results from a national sample of single adults in the United States." *Frontiers of Psychology*. doi:10.3389/fpsyg.2021.619640

Rubel, A.N. and Bogaert, A.F. (2015) "Consensual nonmonogamy: Psychological well-being and relationship quality correlates." *Journal of Sex Research* 52, 9, 961–982.

Rubin, J.D., Moors, A.C., Matsick, J.L., Ziegler, A., and Conley, T.D. (2014) "On the margins: Considering diversity among consensually non-monogamous relationships." [Special Issue on Polyamory]. *Journal für Psychologie* 22, 1, 19–37.

Sanders, L. (2023, February 21) "How many Americans prefer non-monogamy in relationships?" [Blog post]. YouGov. https://today.yougov.com/society/articles/45271-how-many-americans-prefer-nonmonogamy-relationship

Sheff, E. (2020) *Children in Polyamorous Families: Research Findings in Brief.* Create Space [online self-publishing platform].